PORSCHE PASSION

911 HEAVEN AND BEYOND

911 looks to heaven as an RS 'ducktail' frames the legend.

PORSCHE PASSION

911 HEAVEN AND BEYOND

PHOTOGRAPHED & WRITTEN BY LANCE COLE

PEN & SWORD
TRANSPORT

AN IMPRINT OF PEN & SWORD BOOKS LTD.
YORKSHIRE - PHILADELPHIA

First published in Great Britain in 2022 by
Pen and Sword Transport
An imprint of
Pen & Sword Books Ltd.
Yorkshire - Philadelphia

ISBN 978 1 52678 569 5

Typeset by SJmagic DESIGN SERVICES, India.

Printed and bound in India by Replika Press Pvt. Ltd.

Pen & Sword Books Ltd incorporates the imprints of Pen & Sword Books Archaeology, Atlas, Aviation, Battleground, Discovery, Family History, History, Maritime, Military, Naval, Politics, Railways, Select, Transport, True Crime, Fiction, Frontline Books, Leo Cooper, Praetorian Press, Seaforth Publishing, Wharncliffe and White Owl.

For a complete list of Pen & Sword titles please contact

PEN & SWORD BOOKS LIMITED
47 Church Street, Barnsley, South Yorkshire, S70 2AS, England
E-mail: enquiries@pen-and-sword.co.uk
Website: www.pen-and-sword.co.uk

or

PEN AND SWORD BOOKS
1950 Lawrence Rd, Havertown, PA 19083, USA
E-mail: Uspen-and-sword@casematepublishers.com
Website: www.penandswordbooks.com

Contents

Dedication

Auf des leben und werk von Christian Friedrich Carl Alexander, dem letzten Markgrafen von Brandenburg-Anspach, zuletzt von Benham Park, West Berkshire, der seinen Thron aus liebe zur Elizabeth Craven abdankte. Er gab alle seine landereien und titel auf, und kam nach West Berkshire, um pferde zu zuchten. Ich habe eine verbindung zu ihm und der pferden und dem land.

In Memorium

Hans Helmut Otto Albrecht 'John' Sprinzel. October 1930-May 2021. Rally champion, engineer, motor sport figure, sailor, island hopper, renaissance man, gentleman and Porsche 911 driver. Fare-thee-well ancient pelican of the islands.

Acknowledgements

I would like to offer thanks to all those who helped not least with press accreditation and access – notably: Porsche AG; Porsche GB Press Office; Porsche Club GB – notably Chris Sweeting; Dick Lovett Porsche – notably Simon Lismore, and John Sharp; Prescott Hill Climb/ Bugatti Owners Club team; Goodwood (Members Meetings team); Bicester Heritage; Autofarm; Greatworth Classic; Steve Bull Porsche; Josh Sadler; Justin Mather; Donald Peach; Tim Read; Simon Read and Clare Read; Michael Read; the late Dawson Sellar; Alex Rankin; Porsche driving Aussie friends. Thanks to Johan Popp and Derek Popp of the Bavarian/Bohemian originating Popp clan for encouragement many years ago when a familial link existed; Thanks to Robert Baxter for past kindness and automotive encouragement; acknowledgements also for the encouragement given by the late Jeremy Snook at Porsche GB. All photographs by Lance Cole unless stated otherwise. Photographed using Nikon cameras and lenses.

In Pursuit of Porsches – A Conversation

The 1982-built Norbert Singer designed Porsche 956 of Bell/Bellof in modified livery attacks the camera in a blaze of colour and memory. This car broke the Nurbringring record in 6:11.13 minutes during qualifying for the 1000km Sports Car race using its 620hp and ground effect to good advantage. The record stood for thirty five years. Chris Crawford restored the car after its spell in the USA.

Amid the rarefied world of expensive motor cars, sticking one's head over the parapet of so-called perceived wisdom is a risky thing to do. Flash cars are sometimes accompanied by flash egos and even bigger opinions on what is what. Herein, in a personal book of collected Porsche moments I have tried to stick with engineering, design, and enthusiasm, rather than my ego or anyone else's. Amid the world of Porsche there are clans or tribes, purists, fettlers, modifiers and lateral thinkers, 'outlaws' or 'mavericks'. Not all agree and some seem to be in conflict. It was ever thus in the world of marque allegiance and model preference in a world of car clubs.

Maybe purists and less-purists will never agree? But this should not stop either savouring the Porsche passion and its soul. And of course you can have long arguments about what you are going to be pure about, and how pure is pure, and what hierarchical authority gradient will manifest beyond such corporate-speak and club opinions. So the risks inherent in creating a Porsche book are obvious. Surely there are others better qualified, better *known*? 'Who does he think he is?' can go the refrain from the establishment to the interloper, yet without reflection upon who *they* think they are and why they think they know better or how they got there…

My view is, can we not just simply share a passion for Porsche and its engineering and design language? Can I be allowed to air my view through a new lens?

Here it is, ferrous oxide and all.

This is a book of Porsche patina, light falling on curved metal, evocations of scale and sculpture, of colours and paint hues and moments of Porsche amid both the esoteric and the less esoteric. All I have tried to do is capture the spirit and the enthusiasm of all things Porsche and to convey it to you. I hope I have succeeded. I hope you enjoy bathing in Porsche moments and memories. 911 is indeed heaven, but there is something beyond those magical numbers of legend.

Perhaps the current court of public opinion and its refusal to see nuance and analysis, is going to tell us Porschephiles that we should not celebrate a company with certain historical wartime connections – amid claims that some prefer to confabulate into inaccuracy. Read on to find out more about such hypocrisy. I am not bothered about fiefdoms. All I am bothered by is the chance to bathe in the magic of Porsche – however it manifests – be it purist or 'outlaw' in its context. Prejudged Porsche purism and a tightly policed narrow view through the windscreen of Porsche perception are not to be found here in my book, but if they are your thing – good for you.

Was it not Ferry Porsche himself who had stated (in 1969) that the point was not whether a Porsche was air-or water-cooled that was the issue – but whether the cars were any good or not!

Few cars evoke the emotion of a Porsche; few cars have the soul or character of a 911 or a 356. I have tried to communicate that essential essence through the pictures and words herein. 914s, 924s, and 928s get a look-in too.

The Porsche enthusiasm is not a male or macho thing – despite perceptions that it is. Although we can admit that in the 1980s, egos and Turbos ran rampant in Porsches, the truth before and after that era is that women have also driven and owned Porsches. In fact more women own Porsches than other supercar manufacturers can claim as a demographic. A woman named Betty Haig drove and raced her 356 and was instrumental in the early affairs of a Porsche club in Great Britain. If you visit Prescott Hill Climb you will see Laura Wardle howling up the hill in a very pokey 911 Carrera in which she has competed for years.

You might argue that the 928 is a big Germanic 'E-Type' of a sculpture designed by men for men, yet in fact it is only seven and bit inches longer than a full-fat 911and has many curved contours and delicate features. But the rampant long-nose deceives you, as does the technological leap that was its bumper-less style (built-in bumpers as a part of the bodywork were a major 928 design achievement). But Porsches do not follow fashion, they set it. 928 was a supreme act of industrial design by any standards – surely?

I have no shame in being fascinated by Porsche the man. How did Porsche senior, old Ferdinand, go from being a tinsmith's offspring to become an inventor, engineer, designer and global icon? Ferdinand Porsche was a true 'influencer', not some latter-day celebrity idiot with a sense of self-entitlement and little knowledge of life or anything.

What genius channelled through Ferdinand and from him? How and why did all this happen?

Remember, Ferdinand was, over one hundred years ago, creating electric-powered cars and hybrid-powered electro-mechanical cars as the previous century dawned and the Austrian empire – and then the Habsburg monarchy – faded and a new map of Europe was born amid a war that was far from being 'Great' in 1914-1918. From Reichenburg and Bohmisch-Leipa in Northern Bohemia to Gmund Austria, and Stuttgart in Germany, the Porsche and sons journey has been a fascinating one. Ferdinand embraced new thinking and new aerodynamics. His mind was open, and what a mind it was.

In the here and now, my local official Porsche Centre (OPC) is a wonderful place full of enthusiasts, but I have bumped into visitors with unfortunate arrogance and that modern sense of self-entitlement that is so unappealing in woman or man. It is a shame that the brand has become favoured by such classless people of 'high net worth' and poor manners. They are not really car, or Porsche enthusiasts, are they? They are self-enthusiasts. So sod them and let's just stare at Porsches. Thirty five years on from my teenage boyhood obsession that saw me standing outside the then local Porsche dealer (named

Dick Lovett) in Marlborough, and staring through the window at a 911 and a 924 Carrera GT, I am still staring through (much glossier) showroom windows at 911s and more. I know I am not alone in such wanderings of the mind.

There is a Porsche waiting outside the gates of remembrance.

As I cross the countryside in pursuit of Porsches, I drop in at shrines like Autofarm, Steve Bull, Williams Crawford, RPM, Revival-Cars, Charles Ivey, and Greatworth Classics, to name a few. The proprietors just let me stare at Stuttgart steel. At Greatworth's annual enthusiasts' day, the camaraderie amid the soul of the Porsche culture is something special – whatever your net worth. Also just up the road from my home I found Stuttgart Classica which is self-explanatory.

Up at Border Reivers, Tom Fitzsimmons caters both for the Porsche purist and Porsche fan of modified mind. Buried away from the glare of publicity and the London bubble, Border Reivers are custodians of a Porsche culture that you really ought to know about. I wonder if Tom knew Dawson Sellar, the ex-Porsche designer who lived not so many miles away along the Wigtownshire side of the Solway estuary prior to his sad passing? Sellar was a Scot with a hand on the culture of Porsches, dogs, fine whisky, boats, islands and inspired industrial design. He also happened to be a co-founder (with Peter Stevens) of the Royal College of Art's vehicle design unit.

Near Heathrow, pilot-turned-Porsche expert Max Levell (a name that is surely an aviation term in itself) has focused on the delight of the 912 and is fast becoming a purveyor of 912 provenance. 912s are lovely, but you have to *drive* one to get how sweet they are.

From Prescott to Shelsley, from Bicester to Goodwood and beyond onto the rural roads of Great Britain, I have pursued Porsches with my cameras to capture memories. They are parked herein.

One of the highlights of chasing Porsches was Classics at the Castle – a Porsche gathering founded by Fred Hampton who also happens to be 356 Register Secretary at Porsche Club GB. 356s seem have to a bunch of followers who get what 356 is all about – beyond the 911 bubble. I have spotted Hampton all over the place in his 356 – he drives it as it was designed to be.

I got the 356 bug when discovered an old 356 in a barn in Zimbabwe thirty years ago. South Africa has recently yielded up an original, 1966 911 as an S-model factory development prototype (chassis 310001S) that somehow got sold to no less a personage than Hans Hermann and then went off to another life and ended up in South Africa of all places. Bailey Cars have rescued and restored this very rare prototype factory-original 'bitsa' of a pure Porsche prototype – the first 911S chassis and a short-to-long wheelbase official 'mule' it appears.

Racing and rallying are at the heart of Porsche, so to stand in awe at the Le Mans Classics, or at Silverstone, or Prescott, and see Porsches at full speed revving their hearts out, seems appropriate to the long history of Porsche competition and its tutelage.

I am lucky enough to have visited Porsche at Weissach and, to have driven a 959 down the autobahn at above the speed at which Concorde used to hit Vr and rotate off the runway.

To coin a well-worn currently fashionable phrase, it has been a journey.

Over in California, there can be found the famous groups of Porsche modifiers and restorers, amongst them is a man named Matt Hummel who drives a patinated 356 of great character and has a collection of truly original old German cars. Also in California can be found the reimagining of an original Le Mans-competing 356 Gmund aerodynamic coupe – a Cameron Healy/Rod Emory project no less.

Are there are old 356s still secreted away in Cuba? Imagine finding one of those.

Beyond the walls of Stuttgart and the big branding machine of corporate Porsche, their lies the varying degrees of non-conformism that are the likes of Autofarm, Paul Stephens, and the different works of Alois Ruf, Rob Dickinson at Singer, Rod Emory, Tech Art, FVD Brombacher, RPM Technik, Bruce Canepa, and Magnus Walker. Each of these in their own respective manner has added to the external Porsche legend. And have you seen the Jack Olsen 911 Special?

356 purists had best look away from the Emory Motorsports/Momo 356 'evocation' hot rod racer. But I love it. If Emory can make any fading 356 'better' and give it improved brakes, more performance, less emissions and a safer, more comfortable drive amid a build quality that saves an old car from its end, then why not? But you are allowed to disagree, so long as you allow others to see things from their standpoint. Tolerance is far too often a one-side claim made by people with power – providing you agree with them.

Meanwhile Porsche culture and Porsche subculture gets everywhere.

This Porsche thing is an addiction, you see; one that I know you suffer from too. Currently I do not own a Porsche, but an oily rag old one will appear in the windscreen of my consciousness soon. But memories of conducting a 356 and, of driving a 911 in East Africa still perpetuate my dreams. The wail of a flat-six on an African dirt road and the concentration required to stay alive, still flash across my soul in a lucky memory of a driving life. I am so glad it was a Land-Rover I rolled multiple times through the African landscape, not that 911. Still, if the Land-Rover had not landed on its wheels, I might not be here, Land-Rovers without roll cages being rather risky things…

I spent some time with a ratty old 912 and loved it. I met fellow Porschephiles through that.

I was on hand at Prescott to help deliver the Porsche Museum's Bell/Bellof 956 car and grabbed some shots of that epoch making legend. It reeks of its story. The first 'Porsches at Prescott' event was special indeed.

Recently I have taken to a more sedate 'fix' – reading an independent Australian Porsche production named *Duck and Whale*. It is a superb publication and one not be missed if you are of independent and curious mind. Oh, what joy it is to turn such pages. Lee Dean, the publisher of *Duck and Whale*, seems to know what make us tick – Porsches, people and detail. Other excellent Porsche magazines exist; *911 & Porsche World* being another supplier of what I see as a method of Porsche bathing. Websites and forums are alive with varying degrees of separation from 'purism'.

'Early 911' registers and clubs seem huge fun for the forensically minded.

I prefer smaller, more nimble Porsches that are lithe, such as 356 or 912, or short-wheelbase early 911. But I have come to love the old 914/6 (a much underestimated device, contaminated by a prejudged narrative) and also the new Cayman as four-pot powered and of GT six-pot power. The more recent 911 seems too big and too short-nosed to me, but that does not mean I dislike it – after all it still embodies all that is magical about Porsche and its process. But right now, a Cayman seems ideal to me as a personification of the Porsche process. But you may well disagree.

One of the most interesting things about the Porsche culture – or subculture – is the things people do to their Porsches. Now the purist will not agree, but I know many Porsche people who do agree. From purist 'pebble bleach' perfection to 'outlaw' to 'oily rag', Porsche has it all.

Personally I cannot think of anything less interesting or worthy of my time than a totally restored, wiped-out, newly coated vinyl and acrylic 'concourse' restoration that has obliterated a car's life story and psychometry only to replace it with a plastic patina of so-called perfection. But hey, if that is what you want to spend a hundred thousand or more on, then that is your prerogative. What consenting adults do in the privacy of their garages, is their affair, not mine.

I am sure you now realise that this is a personal book and yet a freethinking one. If you do not like my view, please provide your own – being better and in published form of course.

There are front-engined Porsches in this book and I make no apology, for they are excellent cars that you dismiss at your own behest. The 928 must surely now be seen as the triumph of engineering and industrial design that it was and remains. But, of course, 911 is still 'the thing' for many. Of Panamera? Cayenne? Macan? Great cars, but not yet modern classics and not really the essence of the ethos I am aiming for herein. So, like it or lump it, they are not found in this book. Sorry.

Some of the cars on these pages are bright and shiny, but there is always room for the patina and psychometry of that state now known as 'oily rag'.

I have included a photograph of a Taycan in this book because it is so elegant, so pure in its Porsche design language. To me, Taycan's electrickery is another subject – after all, unless the electricity-supplying power station is fuelled on climate friendly non-carbon materials, then as with any electric car, all we have done is move the power generating emissions down the road to the coal-fired power station; this is a truth that marketing neatly side-steps. Hopefully, coal-fired power stations will be outlawed and electric cars can charge up from friendlier sources.

As for simply removing the car's exhaust and claiming green credentials yet plugging into a polluted power grid for a charge, well, you can keep it. Oh, and as for mining the land and now mining the seabed and all the disturbance to nature's order that that entails, in order to source the rare earth minerals like lithium, cadmium, and cobalt to make rechargeable batteries, well it's not so clever, is it? But then, every mobile phone contains such materials and every gallon of petrol needs cobalt in its refining process prior to its combustion and discharge through a cobalt-equipped catalytic convertor. So you cannot win either way.

But the fact remains that Taycan is a glorious celebration of all things engineering amid Porsche, a wonderful design motif of decades of Porsche design that ran from Ferdinand the First, to Erwin Komenda, to Ferry Porsche, thence to Butzi Porsche and on through the likes of top Porsche designers by the names of, Lapine, Mobius, Soderberg, Sellar, Hatter, Lai, Murkett, and onwards to current styling boss Mauer, exterior design director Peter Varga and their colleagues today brilliantly evoke all things Porsche without resorting to retro-Porsche pastiche.

When you climb into any Porsche (including a Taycan) the correctness of it all embraces you immediately; there is a tangible feel and a purpose apparent. There is no denying the sense of occasion. This is the start of the journey before you have even turned the key. The ingredients of this mechanical relationship are defining. I have tried to frame such feelings in this book.

As I have said, this book is an entirely personal collection of Porsche moments and likely to be appreciated by some and, in a social media age of criticism without responsibility, denigrated by others; after all opinions are like car exhausts, everyone has one (unless you are of electric 'perfection'). If you do not like my collection of Porsche photography, then I regret that and do of course look forwards to receiving a review copy of your own book when it is published and has defined the definitive. In the meantime, these images capture what I think is that elusive *character* of Porsche. True, they are in the main British-filmed photographs but a Porsche is a Porsche whatever its number plate. I have scattered a handful of official Porsche images (as approved for editorial use) across my selection. Sadly, Covid put an end to my Porsche road-trip across America.

No matter, here, across many events and locations are images from a Porsche bathe, a mindful immersion in the forms, scales, sculptures, and sounds of all things Porsche. Ah, Porsche bathing: mindful Porsche – how nice. Only a book can reach such parts –apart from a Porsche itself of course.

Having grown up surrounded by old Saabs, old Citroens, old Land-Rovers, old MGs, and the occasional old Porsche (there was an orange 911 2.2 on our drive at one stage of my childhood), car design became passion for me. I learned to drive on a Fordson Major tractor, 1949 VW Beetle, a Saab 96, and a Land-Rover Series One. I mastered the art of rallying the Beetle on mud and going sideways and backwards simultaneously, by the age of sixteen. I drove a Porsche for the first time when I was eighteen. I have never forgotten that moment, because as with the VW and the Saab, there was that innate connection to the mechanism of the car and the driving of it. The Porsche had a soul and it was obvious.

Other members of my family have worked in the motor industry in several countries and like them I too suffer from the addiction to classic cars and classic aircraft. Porsche of Stuttgart looms large. Silesia holds a special place in my heart for private reasons and an ancestor came from the Swabian/ Bavarian border, so maybe that is where the link in part comes from. And I wonder if the mesmerising girl from Trutnov who once traversed my consciousness and who liked Porsches will ever read this.

The pattern of the past is always there, but not many are in touch with it.

Architecture gives you a house to live in and learn to love; Porsche design gives you a car to drive and cherish. It really is that simple and yet so clever. Maybe only an old Saab, an old Lancia or Alfa Romeo, or old Citroën or old Bristol can come close to a Porsche in terms of emotional involvement and sheer character.

Porsche fanatics are a tribal demographic, and are of many different social types. Some are 'purists', certain Porschephiles will not tolerate anything post-1963, post-1975, or post-1986, some accept water-cooling, some do not. I am not alone in not being uncritical of Porsche and to me the newer 911 generation is, to my subjective taste, too short-nosed and too digital, but that's just my opinion, not an opinion as fact. Your opinion will view a different partiality.

Yet *Luftgekühlt* (air-cooled) remains an obsessive ethos but people forget that it is the oil – as oil-flow circulating inside an airflow-cooled engine that plays a major role in cooling the engine's forged and cast metal/alloy components more than a blast of vented-in air.

Of horizontally opposed 'Boxer' engines – first invented by Mercedes engineers rather than Porsche, yet made famous by Porsche (and Citroën) long before Subaru used them, we might ask, is that engine configuration and mechanism a 'religion' that cannot be challenged? Of course not: if something better comes along, embrace it – a Porsche philosophy for sure.

But how far do we go with change for the sake of it? To activate the Taycan's on-board digital systems, you have to speak to it – yes, speak to it. What if it says 'No' – or '*Nein, wir haben einen technischen problem*'.

An unfortunate legal row recently developed via Erwin Komenda's descendants' hands over the works, effects and rights of old Ferdinand's right hand man Komenda in design terms. Komenda heavily influenced Porsche car body design in the late 1930s through to the late 1950s, but was he not influenced by 1930s design trends himself? Most car designers were. But Komenda innovated that ellipsoid, sculpted rear-end that defined the early Porsches and remains a key design ingredient at Porsche today. But this does not necessarily mean all Porsches owe him an acknowledgement – does it? Porsche have now given this design motif a marketing term and called it the (historical) 'fly-line'. How clever, but do you really care what it's called?

Claim and counter claim over who drew what are normal in car design. Latterly Porsche very unfortunately cropped Komenda from sight in its use of the famous photograph of the first 356 prototype with Ferdinand, Ferry, and Erwin all standing beside 'their' car. However Porsche's own *Christophorus* magazine categorically stated in 1966, that the generic Porsche form was basically Erwin Komenda's work, but that is vague enough to fit, is it not?

All I know is that, at Porsche, Komenda was a vital contributor, a co-founder as Paul Frère called him in print: Komenda was a brilliant and consummate designer and body engineer who deserves his credit, but so, too, do others. And what you design for your employer is their property, is it not – unless you take out your own registration upon work funded that employer? It is a legal nightmare.

Ferdinand's son F.A.E 'Ferry' Porsche heavily influenced the 356 say some, while other accounts say it was all his work. Ferdinand Senior's grandson 'Butzi' drew the original 901/911 (out of a design study for a four-seat 356 derivative) and also penned his lovely 904, and more. Others are better qualified to define how much other people were involved, or if Komenda played one role or another role or influence while working for the beloved brand. Why can't we all agree that they were all bloody clever and be thankful for that?

A defining power in later Porsche design was the Latvian-American design leader Anatole 'Tony' Lapine, another northern European émigré who gravitated to Stuttgart. Wolfgang Möbius was a Lapine team member and greatly influenced the timeless form of the 928. Richard Soderberg played a major role in Porsche design, as did the Scot Dawson Sellar, and more recently the Dutchman Haarm Lagaay (Laagij) who carved out Porsche in its more modern era and his contribution should not be underestimated.

Reinhold Schreiber, Eberhard Brose, Ernst Bolt, Sigi Notacker, and Hans Braun were key members of the Porsche 1970s design studio amid styling, sketching, clay modelling and body engineering functions.

Other names of designers from as far afield as Hong Kong (Pinky Lai), Turkey (Hakan Saracoglu), the USA (Grant Larsson) and Brits like Steve Murkett and A.R. 'Tony' Hatter (993-stylist and now senior design and style leader at the Porsche studio) are all key strands of Porsche design language. All their contributions can be found in the modern Porsche story. Lai is interesting because he was not a northern European, so he brought a new view from fresh eyes and time has proven his 996 design to be both timeless and rather special. As for Michael Mauer, the current design boss? Hail the chief and his vision of new with old but never as pastiche. Mauer used to design for Saab and now he designs for Porsche. To say that I am envious would be to put it mildly.

For some, the 911 is Porsche, yet for others, there is a wider Porsche. I hate people being nasty about the 914 – because it is a superb piece of Porsche industrial design and it *drives*, especially as a 914/6. Personally, I fancy an oily-rag 356 or earlier 911, but I can see that 924, 944, and 928 were wonderful cars full of brilliant engineering of the Porsche process. If you want to slag off the Boxster, that is your affair. Yet Boxster touched the core of the Porsche ethos and is a very good car.

Water-cooling and the 996? A difficult biscuit to bite on for some, but you may disagree. Think of the new converts to Porsche that Boxster and 996 have created. A friend of mine has just purchased an immaculate, used, dark blue Boxster for less than the price of a new Dacia Sandero. He says it has brought huge joy to his life and shown him what driving is again. What about picking up a well-serviced 996 for under £15,000? You still can. What joy! And the 996 is wearing rather well into its modern classic status, is it not?

911 may be 'king' but what of 912 – original or that later short-lived 912E of America? Actually, they are both great drivers' cars with even more telepathy in the steering than a 911. Okay, a 911 2.7RS would trounce a 912 in the desirability stakes, but 912s were denounced for years. What snobbery did this? 912s can be seen herein because I and my Porsche friends love them: 912 – so pure.

Is there really such a huge gulf between driving a Boxster or Cayman and a 'proper' 911? Of course not – a difference, *yes*, but on the sliding scale of perceptions, can we please remember that a Boxster, or a Cayman, *are* Porsches. You do not agree – oh well. *Fahren in seiner schonster form* – to coin a previous Porsche piece of marcomms blurb.

To my mind, the Cayman now seems to embody all the Porsche essentials in a more chuckable driver's package. How interesting to note a return to six cylinders over the recently favoured four. A Gentian Blue, GT4 manual, for me, please, Porsche. But no gold-hued wheels, thank you.

Of course, Porsche has become the Porsche A.G. Zuffenhausen, Stuttgart branding machine. Today's Porsche brand and Porsche family, headed by Ferdinand Senior's grandson (Ferry's son) Dr Wolfgang Heinz Porsche, are joint guardians of a precious cargo. But an Austro-Hungarian-Bohemian enclave is where Porsche originated. Indeed, in the 1970s, the Austrian government paid Porsche to design a new Austrian car that could have become an Austro-Porsche-framed brand. It did not reach production. Way back in 1890-something, there were emerging cars of 'Austro' lineage and also car marques of a distinct identity, yet which have faded along the road to globalised branding.

For me, Porsche, notably the 356 and the 1970s 911s, have always seemed to be to the essential elements of central European car design. Oh, and throw in Tatra and Ledwinka, Jaray, Rumpler, Austro-Daimler, Laurent and Klemin, Lohner, N.S.U., Praga, Skoda, and Steyr. For Austro-Bohemia gave rise to automotive genius. Old Ferdinand Porsche became its scion and its surviving manifestation of Bohemian brilliance.

Mentioning central Europe allows me to cast off on a Porsche point: contrary to what you might now assume from ill-informed public opinion, Porsche, the man, his son, the men, and their cars, were not 'posh', neither were they 'German' nor were they 'Nazi' – as themed in the modern geo-political or senses or contexts. In fact, Porsche senior came from humble origins and a lineage of Bohemia amid Austro-Hungary long before the map of Europe was re-drawn to create today's Germany, or Czechoslovakia, the Czech Republic, Slovakia, Austria, or Poland.

Porsche is not quite as 'German' as you might perceive. Austro-Bohemia, Silesia, and old kingdoms and cantons amid an Austro-Hungarian arena of the regions, gave rise to an engineering tradition that manifested between Prague, Vienna, Munich, Stuttgart, and Berlin, long before two world wars ripped up the old order and cast down in spilt blood and treasure a new age and, bizarrely, a new engineering excellence that touched automobiles and aeroplanes, and many other things too.

In the unlikely event that you do not know, Ferdinand Porsche was born in and of the Austro-Hungarian sphere of registration; he was then to a become Czech, then an Austrian-German citizen. He was born of old Bohemia's DNA and therefore not 'German' to start with. What we today recognise as Germany and as German, are of course twentieth century constructs and do not really explain the land, the DNA, the politics and the history of that ancient and uncertain arena.

Some less than forensic claims have been made about founder Ferdinand Porsche and his work (as ordered) for the post-1933 Nazi regime and many confabulated narratives of fashionable inaccuracy at the court of public opinion now exist. Yes, he did design Hitler's car, but did so long before war erupted and did so because he was ordered to do so. Old man Porsche was not a politically active Nazi and neither was his son. And after all, it's not as though he designed the rockets and missiles as weapons of war that then took America to the moon after their creator (von Braun) 'became' a much-lauded American citizen and praised in the streets just twenty-five years after the end of the war in which his machines of mass destruction built from conscripted labour took part against the land of the free.

Space rocket man von Braun's boss was a general who the British detained on war criminal charges at a prison camp in Wales for many months (along with some of his top men), but suddenly he was freed without the intended charge and sent off with his experts to deepest America to help the missile and rocket programme that led to the Moon. Oh, and swept-wing airliners and military aircraft were also, shall we say, 'inherited' from the evils of Nazi-funded research that found itself in America after 1945.

No charges were brought against Ferdinand Porsche by the Allied powers after 1945. Indeed, he was given an official document clearing him of any complicity in war crimes and given paperwork stating that no charges were to be brought and then was a free man. He was subjected to the claims of a former employee who it is alleged had his own record and such defamatory claims were soon dismissed. The French tried some manoeuvres out upon him, but that failed too and he was formally cleared.

So Ferdinand Porsche's own detention and freeing in Europe without charge or censure really ought not to be subject to the confabulation that some commentators have created. Aircraft maker W. Messerschmitt was allegedly detained and told to pay retributions, but people quite happily run about in his bubble cars without embarrassment. It's a strange old world, is it not?

If you are going to fall for fashionable Porsche brand and family knocking, then you had better get your facts right, and explain, if connection to post-1933 German or Nazi industrial output was so 'evil', how come millions, yes, *millions* of citizens of the world, notably of Great Britain, and the United States of America (both nations of Judaeo-Christian practice) did not have a problem purchasing and owning the VW Beetle – the so-called 'Hitler's car' as designed by Porsche. Nor did the 1960s-70s American, British, French, (or others) mind being mobilised by the Beetle, nor the VW Camper Van, that emerged from such origins. Think of the multi-cultural holidays and the conceptions that have taken place in VW vans! No condemnation of their VW-based happenings, are obvious in the court of public narrative. Ford's V8 engine was reputedly built by the Nazis at the Ford Cologne engine plant right up to early 1942 and used in various German campaigns not least the Russian incursion. But no one says a word now.

The esteemed motoring writer L.J.K. Setright once had a go at Porsche and his wartime doings with Hitler's cars, engines, tanks, etcetera. Ok, fair enough and as a proud Jew, maybe he felt he had the right given the evil that was once apparent in Nazi actions. And did he attack BMW, or Mercedes-Benz, or NASA, using similar claims? Setright had a pop at Porsche – yet did so as a driver and admirer of certain Japanese cars with origins in the industrial output of old Japan. No conflict there then …

So it might be an idea to climb down off the moral high horse if you are thinking of attacking the Porsches and their origins, their works or the brand. There are plenty of daily, consumable and scientific items in the technology of our lives that stemmed from wartime Germany, its science and its Nazi funding yet which were absorbed into American and British life and society. And after all, a current grand prix driver who says a lot about the evils of discrimination is quite happy to take millions in salary from another Stuttgart-based company that built or supplied wartime weapons of mass destruction for the Nazi regime. But hey, at least he does not drive a Porsche.

Oh, and I note a certain car company from Munich that built wartime aircraft engines is hugely popular in America and Great Britain with people of many faiths, creeds and colours, yet with seemingly little concern about its record 1939-1945. The fact that British Bristol Company Ltd motor cars had close engineering and design links to BMW engineering from the late 1930s onwards and beyond 1945, never seems to bother anyone, does it?

The hypocrisy of the anti-Porsche historical narrative is obvious, and that is without citing how swept-wing airliners, Deltoid jet fighters, chemical processes, synthetic materials and fuels, diesel engines, railway locomotives, resins, sound technology, and malaria drugs, to name just a few of the things that the Allies re-branded as their own having 'liberated' them from the Nazi regime in Germany that had either invented them or inherited them from the pre-1933 Germany amid that nation's incredible lode of science. It was no less a figure than Eisenhower (himself of extracted German DNA) who described such German science as 'twenty-five years ahead' – just in case you did not know. Oh, and Churchill called it 'perverted science' – but that did not stop the British and the Americans scouring Germany in 1945-1946 for all the secrets of its advanced technology and to spirit them and their creators away at Allied taxpayers' expense.

'Operation Paperclip' is where you need to start to discover that the Allies, and notably the Americans (and the British, the French and the Russians), were quite happy to scoop up the men who had invented the tools of Hitler's war trade and then to re-purpose them and their inventions for their own use and advancement in technological and monetary terms across the decades since 1945, in what is often termed a 'golden age' of American or British technology.

The Germans have not wanted to discuss the war for decades whereas the British still seem obsessed with working out how they won it despite the odds and their enemy's efficiency. In 1945, hundreds of German, Nazi, and non-Nazi inventors, designers, engineers and experts of weaponry were gathered in London at the British taxpayers' expense to be kept just yards from the impact sites of the various weapons of mass destruction such men had created. Thereupon, the genius of such enemy minds was sifted for the advancement of Allied science. No one has made a fuss. Yet Ferdinand Porsche still gets it in the neck for designing the Volkswagen car that mobilised much of the world and remained in production in South America until recently.

A classic scene. A black 911 races up Prescott in a blur of power and style. Ian Wadsworth pushed the 1974 991 with 2,993cc hard up the hill into the Esses, to achieve a best time of 50.84 – only just slower than David Dyson's two 48.86 and 50.45 second runs with his newer 3,800cc 911 that took 1st place. The Class 2 record was held by Bob Mortimer in a 911RS at 46.26seconds in 2007.

Sapphire Blue dream machine. 911 heaven as captured on the go.

You might think that the Delta wing was a British invention first made real by the British on the Avro Vulcan, and then seen on Concorde. Well, however wonderful those two aircraft and their designers were, the truth is that the Delta wing was invented by Alexander Lippisch in 1930 and test flown at Berlin Templehof 1931, long before Hitler rose to power in 1933.

You might not know that the leading diesel railway locomotives of 1950s and 1960s Britain were direct lifts of wartime German technology copied straight from German plans but rebranded to shield the public from such truth at government order, just a decade from the end of the war. An American locomotive was of similar provenance.

So you can see that somehow the choosing of targets of protest is now highly selective to many people – not least as they queue up outside clothing shops to buy cheap clothes produced in alleged tropical modern-slavery conditions by children in toxic surroundings for low wages with few rights.

Yet mention a certain German supercar manufacturer named Porsche and suddenly accusations fly about claims of working for the wrong people. It is both a hypocrisy and a madness of the 'narrative'. No nation, no culture, no major religion, is free of error. So, it is time we took a more rational view – but as that does not fit the current narrative – the current 'spin' of geo-political social science, my dissent may lead to attack or 'cancel culture' upon me for daring to suggest nuance and historical forensics.

What has all this history got to with Porsche? Answer, a lot, because German science, engineering and design was years ahead of the British, the French, or the Americans and so too was Porsche science and engineering thinking. Hence the cars and the tractors were rather interesting too. Therein lay the forensic thinking and process of application of Porsche Senior and his son.

If you want to know where the science of car or road vehicle aerodynamics really took off, try 1930s Germany and the Stuttgart Research Institute of Automotive Engineering (now part of the Stuttgart University). The names of Wunibald Kamm (Swiss-born), and of Baron Reinhard von Koenig-Fachsenfeld (von Fachsenfeld built upon the Austrian Paul Jaray's aerodynamic car studies) led the field in automotive aerodynamics from cars to motorcycles. Kamm found himself 'invited' to America just after the end of the war – where he would go on to a Professor's role in American engineering. We ought to mention Frederick Lanchester and his British pioneering aerodynamic works, but Stuttgart, not Paris nor London, was the centre of automotive aerodynamics long before the subject became so fashionable. Porsche was there.

Ferdinand Porsche and Erwin Komenda both used all that they could learn from aerodynamics and Porsche's amazing be-winged world land speed record cars created from 1934-1938 deployed such research. Those cars proved the point that Stuttgart knew what aerodynamics were and Porsche had learnt and applied the theories to his pre-1939 cars – notably

Who said 996 was a 'lesser' 911? 50 FAB is a lovely Aqua Blue 996 Turbo of 2003 vintage that was sporting some very nice wheels as it blasted away from Bicester. In the background, a red 911 homes in. Time for a TCAS alert!

those for Auto-Union, Daimler, Wanderer, and the very first total 'Porsche design bureau' car concept that was the Berlin-Rome Type 64 Streamliner of 1939.

By now it must be obvious that I have no problem with praising Porsche the company and the man who started it all. You have to wonder if others' jealousy of polymath Porsche genius has its own agenda? For clarity, I have taken no money, nor expenses, from any German company in the creation of this book – although I did use a Japanese camera which we must assume to be free of historical corporate taint, malpractice, wartime excesses, or past or modern slavery.

So let's hear no more selective Porsche-bashing. If you want to criticise or punish them, apply your analysis to all others too.

What the Porsche family and their chosen men created was unique and remains so. It is beyond a design language or engineering excellence, it is more than a process, it is an utterly superb blending of engineering, industrial design and driving. In the 356, we can safely say that Porsche changed driving; it altered the practice and perception of the sports car and opened a new gateway to motoring in a new form. Apart from the occasional Bugatti, Voisin,

Hispano-Suiza, or such exotic marque of limited production, few cars prior to 356 had delivered such motoring magic to the car buying public.

The Porsche process began at the 'Porsche Bau' – the design bureau of the 1930s. Porsche Senior died in 1951 just as his and his son's 356 was becoming the first Porsche-branded car. But the origins lay in four decades of genius from the old man and his followers.

Even more decades on, the Porsche process has resulted in a Porsche culture, even in a subculture. With that realisation, here goes with a visual immersion in the forms and colours of Porsche and an essence, as captured across several seasons of Porsche moments. In these cars, you can see their soul.

Unless stated, all the photographs stem from my lens (just a few are from the Porsche archive). I hope you enjoy the journey. I don't do corporate-speak, but as they say, the optics seem clear; herein lies a Porsche passion, mine and I hope, yours. We start with a primordial Porsche looming large in the windscreen of our remembrance amid the afterwards and the before of Bohemia.

Lance Cole
West Berkshire via Silesia

356 on the fly: a pure Porsche moment captured at the Greatworth Classic Porsche enthusiasts meeting – which is one of the best for cars and camaraderie. Can't you just hear that engine?

Prescott and Porsche. Cayman S with Darren Slater at the wheel howls up the hill during a Prescott round of the 2018 Petro-Canada Lubricants Porsche Club National Hillclimb Championship. Small, nimble, very pointy on the road, Cayman is a delight of a Porsche that is not a 911.

Above: 924 delight. A superb red 1982 924 hustles up the hill. Driver: Stuart Maclean: Car: 924 2.-0-litre prepared by Victoria Garage, Richmond, Yorkshire. All these years on, 924 still looks like a brilliant piece of industrial design.

Right: Light falling on Stuttgart metal. The late-1959 'oily rag' and wonderfully real, 356 in all its patina scuttles away from a Porsche gathering at Greatworth Classics.

Above: Under a suitable sky, this stunning 1998 vintage 993 GT 2 Evo of Paul McLean/GT Classics was one of the highlights of the first 'Porsches at Prescott' gathering. It may be static, but it oozed the Porsche vibe in its design, wings, dive-plates and BBS wheels. McLean is an air-cooled enthusiast, to put it mildly.

Left: Classic silhouette as a Carrera RS slides by in black and white.

Gulf Blue and orange – pure unadulterated Porsche aura. Note this 3-litre 911's flared arches, front bumper valance intake and the rear wing. Usually driven by Chris Stone or Ross Stone but on this occasion with veteran hillclimber David Franklin at the helm.

Black script down the side of an RS is rarer than blue or red. 'FGV' hunkers down as the power builds and the rear end squats. Flat-six symphony.

Right: Goodwood Members Meeting and two early narrow-body classic 2.0-litre flat-six 911s show off their respective rumps. Note the 911 script badge on the back of SXI 901 – a 901-series car built in mid-1964 from the first three months of full 911 production (so a rare type 300) and believed to be the 180th car built and originally supplied to coachbuilders D'Ieteran; more recently a Historika car. Behind, JUX 441D was British registered in late 1966.

Below: Seen in all its purity this early 928 captures the Lapine/Mobius design work in all its harmony. Surely 928 should now be seen for the design great that it was and remains?

Josh Sadler was here. Autofarm badge affixed, engine tweaked and modified using interesting modified components. In fact this was originally a Bob Watson modified 3.5-litreFlat-six and is seen at rest in all its wonderment. This car sports a twin-plug distributor too and a 3.5-litre punch. The car has its HTP papers and a sort of 'RSR' spec with modified camshafts, pistons and has Porsche's in-built harmonic balancers that benefitted the magnesium crankcase's life expectancy. Not to be confused with Sadler's former other 911 – the factory development 1969 S/T that also once wore 'VRC' plates.

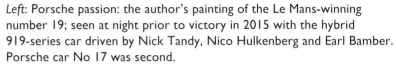

Left: Porsche passion: the author's painting of the Le Mans-winning number 19; seen at night prior to victory in 2015 with the hybrid 919-series car driven by Nick Tandy, Nico Hulkenberg and Earl Bamber. Porsche car No 17 was second.

Below left: Le Mans en bleu. The author's atmospheric night time painting of a 1970s Porsche 917K at Le Mans. Porsche has won Le Mans 19 times and has dozens of class wins to add to that tally.

Below right: Static art: Porsche alloy wheel captured by the author's hand.

Earlier Cayman in red with upgraded wheels and that stance that can only say Porsche.

Kevin Clarke (at the wheel) is Secretary of 914 Register at Porsche Club Gb and rightly so. He has owned twelve 914s and this is his 914/6 – which means it is super, smaller, lithe little Porsche with all the character of a fine design now matured. Quite why so many people were snotty about the 914 seems strange to contend. Here was everything of the older pre-911 Porsche ethos. True, 914s rusted, but in terms of design and driving, this was an advanced car, yet one to be over shadowed by fashion, opinion and a narrative. Only now are people finally beginning to realise what a Porsche precursor this car was. Here lay another view.

The open road and a 356 B T6 Cabriolet of 1963 – arguably an 'ultimate' incarnation of 356 with perfect poise as it speeds away from Prescott in a blur of blue. An evocative moment on the Porsche journey.

1

Primordial Porsche

Porsche and patina captured in badge brightwork.

356 – magic numbers and essence of Porsche's thoroughbred that seems to reek of old Bohemia and the shapes of the 1930s, of Ledwinka, Jaray, Gerin, Ganz, Sason, Bertoni, Geddes, Voisin, Bugatti, Lancia, and more clearly of Komenda and of course manifesting as a fast-backed lithe little car of elegance yet minimalist form. There is no bling, no excess, nor ego in this car.

This is genesis, the laying down of ancient DNA in a new strain yet being a new child with the shape and guts of something old and well-engineered. This is Porsche purity and therefore, I call it the primordial (*ursprünglich*) Porsche that led to that afterwards of the before.

356 started it all and was in a sense, the 'fungal' or spore origin of Porsche as we know it from 911 and beyond.

356 shouts its own origins and its excellence at you. It seethes, it actually smells of a distinct character, a melange of metals, leather, and hand-hewn

materials that amalgamate into a lovely little air-cooled device that burbles and scuttles along and about with delight on main roads and minor roads. Despite appearances, 356 is not small inside and even the tall can fit.

Stemming from those pre-war racers, the road-race cars, the prototypes, the Type 60 and 64 cars, here lies the original.

356: the thoroughbred.

Based on a drawing number of 356:00.105, Ferry Porsche led engineers Rabe and Rupilius, body engineer Komenda, and designer Reimspiess; they created a sweet little, open-topped, tubular-framed, roadster body with a sculpted, curved style, faired-in lights and a new design of one-piece integrated bumpers. Yet before long, it would be a production monocoque body devoid of its prototype's underlying tubular support chassis, and soon one with a coupé top and aerodynamics considered.

The engine design team included project directors Hans Tomola and Klaus von Bucker; design and development men included: Leopold Janstche (an ex-Tatra employee) as leader, with Robert Binder, Horst Marchart, Helmutt Rombols, Hans Honick and Helmuth Bott. Ferdinand Piech led the engine design function and a certain young Hans Mezger was to join in 1956 and become vital to the design and would go on to fame for many 911 engine variations.

So Porsche's later 911 engine guru, Hans Mezger – who had joined Porsche in 1956 and soon worked in the racing car engine department – notably on the 1.5-litre eight-cylinder engine, was to make a contribution to the early development of Porsche engines prior to his 911 flat-six fame.

Three other significant 356 team members included: Porsche's first true sales agent, Alfred Prinzing; the engineer and 356 production manager Hans Klauser (who had joined Porsche in 1933 as an apprentice designer); the company's first-ever dedicated race mechanic and also test driver Hermann Priem, who performed several factory roles in the early 356 years including as an after sales customer-care servicing expert; Herbert Linge who had joined Porsche in 1948, was involved in the twelve-man team which built the first 356, and also performed multiple roles in the service-field for the company. He went on to fame in the Porsche racing department.

As 356 became a production reality, other names would join the small team in the early 1950s. This included Leopold Schmid, the engineer who would soon lead the design office. Helmuth Bött joined the company in a junior role but quickly rose to lead the road test and prototype development department. Hans Tomola, the engine specialist, would soon also join Porsche. Ernst Führmann had joined Porsche in the post-war days. Klaus von Rucker arrived at Porsche early on but would latterly work for BMW in Munich as the decade of the 1960s dawned. Ferdinand Piech would become ever-more powerful in the evolving Porsche story, and had the power-base to get his way.

By late 1951, Ferry Porsche had even employed a clay modeller – Heinrich Klie – to bring life to the design/styling ideas of the team. He rarely gets a mention in the Porsche story and few know of him. Decades later he would shape the Porsche 914.

Amid the early 1950s competition era of early Porsches, the likes of Claus von Rucker and Huschke von Hanstein were instrumental in the technical and competition/events departments respectively. All that they saw and learned was passed down into the 356 as it developed (the 550s/718s, and 'Spyders' being a parallel channel).

The aristocrat, Fritz 'Huschke' von Hanstein 'the racing baron' had raced cars since the 1930s (he won the Mille Miglia in a BMW 328) and knew Ferdinand Porsche. He joined the Porsches in 1951 – soon to be a roving PR and brand ambassador nearly up to the 1970s, and of course a Porsche driver. He achieved fame driving the Porsche 550 Spyder lightweight racer and won a class at Le Mans in a 356A (with Herbert Linge).

Formula One driver Wolfgang Graf Berghe von Trips (sometimes called 'Taffy' by his motorsport friends) of Schloss Hemmersbach was another Porsche racer, owner and essential contributor to the Porsche legend whom today we are encouraged to obscure because being of such class is politically incorrect and likely to offend the 'woke' brigade. But the upper classes of Germany and Austria took to the 356 and the fact that its creator was the trade class offspring of a tinsmith was utterly irrelevant.

All Porsche history is apparent as you climb down into the 356, that first true, mass-production Porsche device; sliding in over the sill and into the snug command post, the view through the narrow windscreen aperture is inspiring. Here you connect with the car as mechanical device and iteration of your command. Leather, chrome fittings, straps, toggles, switches and knobs, all expertly engineered. You can smell the pure engineering.

Once you have started up, warmed the oil, and released the brakes, move off and get going, the car goes where you think it to go. The steering tells you what is passing under the front wheels. The engine asks you to be its captain. Soon you are scything the little insect along and if it is the larger-engined 356, that turns into driving requiring more process aforethought.

This is the car that changed driving and delivered a new sensation through its pedals and steering wheel.

Being in that cabin was special. Today we forget just how much the 356 improved the act of driving and created a sports car legend: being rear-engined was not the anomaly it seems today. Rear-engined cars were all the rage way back then. Who can forget the Hillman Imp, the Renault Dauphin, or the Chevrolet Corvair.

Oh, the joy of placing the 356 correctly in the correct gear at the correct point on the road, and making it bound along like a snappy dog with longer legs. A terrier of a car? This car would beget 911 – itself a prancing Weimaraner of car, and in later form, no canine analogy applies, because RS and GT-series became cheetahs.

The initial 1950 Zuffenhausen-built production 356 cars had 1,086cc engines of 40hp and they used stock VW KdF cable actuated brakes. By the mid1950s, the 356 had been refined into a 'new' version of itself, thence to benefit from the later 356 'Carrera' model line with light alloy bonnet and rear lid, also established itself as a high-power GT of 115hp and a detuned 100hp Luxe variant that was less frenetic.

1958 saw the 1300 engine phased out and updates including a ZF-made steering wheel (no longer a VW device). Soon, 356 had 1,588cc, almost 100bhp and a higher compression ratio at 9.5:1.

The 'Carrera' branding and technical specifications were first applied to the 356-1500GS/Carrera and as such used the 356A 1300 bodyshell and components as its base. Apart from the engine, bigger tyres and bucket seats, this road and race use car was almost indistinguishable from the base 356 A-series car. 1600 GS would soon follow.

First applied to the 356 and cited as the 1500 GS/547/1 engine, the 'Carrera' badge referred to the Mexican road race of *La Carrera Panamerica* and was transposed to a faster, better handling 356 specification branding, first seen in 1955. Only two original 356 A 1500 GS Carrera had come to Britain by 1956. But soon, all over the world, the 356B Carrera 2 was to be an essential road tool of the time.

The developed 356s were to be the 356B (with a T5 specification nomenclature as 60bhp N, Normal, 75bhp S Super and the 90bhp S90). By 1960, Koni shock absorbers and modified anti-roll bars all improved the handling.

The young Dr Ing Ernst Fuhrmann was the man behind the development of Carrera. The target for Fuhrmann's racing-derived engine was 100bhp at 70bhp per litre. The suggested engine was an over-square four-cam instead of single-cam.

The 356 engine would develop into a range that would be rationalised by 1962-model year with the 1600, 1600s and S-90 engines replaced by the 1600c (75bhp) and 1600SC engine that would produce 95bhp at a more useful 5,800rpm.

Porsche added to the 356 in the B series, the 1,966cc engine, and in a four-cam 2000GS model iteration. GS as 1600 and as 2000 was for the competitive driver. Essentially, the 2000 was an enlarged 1600-type engine of 130bhp that could also be taken to around 150bhp/155bhp (at 6,500rpm) depending on specification and tune. The 1963 356 C gained a larger rear windscreen aperture for better visibility. The dashboard was extended into a vestigial centre console that housed a radio. More power and more luxury dominated.

Was this where and when Porsche took itself upmarket – as the market changed?

Porsche's men from the 356/550/718 era had laid down the ethos of Porsche rally and race success. The 'greats' included Edgar Barth, Jean Behra, Constantin Berkheim, Joakim Bonnier, Fritz Huschke von Hanstein, Hans Herrman, Hans Klauser, Herbert Linge, Peter Mueller, Richard von Frankenburg, Prince von Metternich, Wolfgang von Trips, Dan Gurney and we should not forget that Stirling Moss also drove for Porsche, notably in the 718RS61.

From such exploits and from the 356 grew the next varietal of Porsche's growth spurt – 911 and all that flowed therefrom. But it is here in the essence, in the primordial Porsche that was 356 that the amazing story began. As light falls on those complex curves and perfect design shines, we understand why and how. This car was the magic of the old man and his son manifested as a defining act, a DNA thoroughbred that sired a stable of winners.

Since then, the lineage and the essence have not been diluted, just modified.

The 1939 Berlin-Rome streamliner design by Porsche and Komenda on VW underpinnings. The first 'Porsche' design from the Porsche Bau prior to formation of the brand post 1946. Porsche perfection of form.

The Bohemian, Ferdinand Anton Porsche (1875-1951) founder, genius and defining influence on 20th Century car design but born in 1875. A tinsmith's son who created a global design and engineering legend. He was gone by early 1951, but his legacy will last for ever.

Porsche aerodyne design of 1939 for Daimler-Benz of Stuttgart to challenge the World Land Speed record yet which was cancelled as victim of history and war.

356 scuttling towards the camera in a blast of patina amid the psychometry of an original car and its long story.

The 'tumblehome' hull curve of the 356 sculpture captured on the fly as she hastens away oozing style and history.

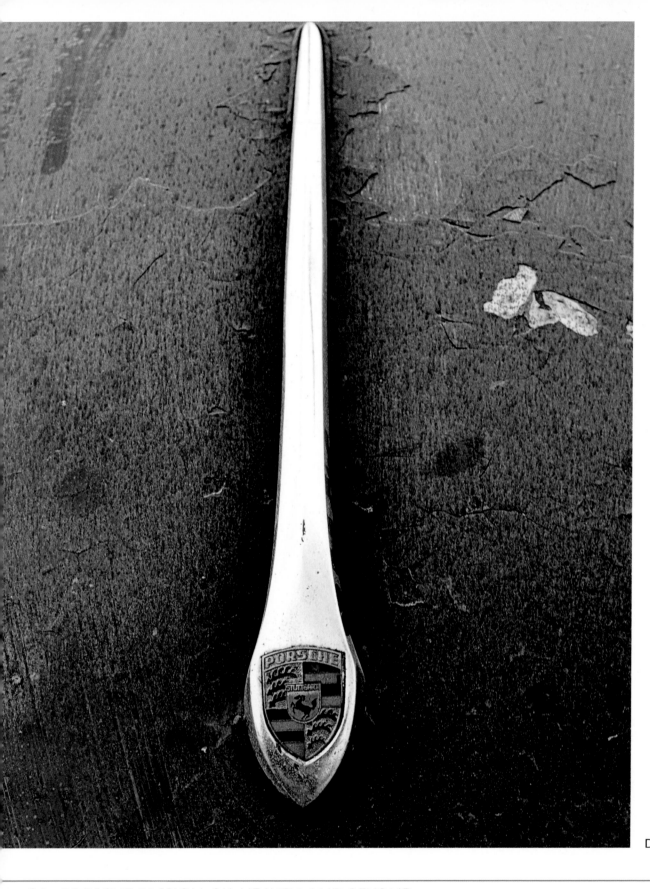

Delightful detail of this 356: the badge that means so much.

Right: You might want to restore it, but others do not: thankfully.

Below: Sculpted details of design perfection.

Age shall not weary the original car. 356 up close and personal.

What can we say? Maybe only restoration is the answer when things have gone this far.

A 1959 era dashboard of this car. Bakelite, steel, tin, chrome, glue, and an aura of originality.

A later 356 interior oozes the hallmarks of refined design from Porsche.

Without its bumper, 951 XUW shows off those lovely ellipsoid vents.

Porsche passion: the wonderfully restored 411 YUH scuttles away from the Classic Motor Hub at Bibury in another Porsche moment beyond 911 heaven. 356C heaven — unless you are a pre-A, split-screen, or bent-screen fancier of course.

The same car captured in its perfection of form. This was design that was correct and classy from every angle. The work of Ferry Porsche with reputed input from Erwin Komenda, 356 set the runes for 1950s–1960s fastback design. We might argue that only Pininfarina's Lancia Aurelia GT rivalled the 356 for scale, sculpture, and overall design perfection. Today, this 356 is both perfect and timeless in its design language. Somehow "outlaw" 356s do not quite hit the same gold spots – do they? From 356 to 911 in terms of styling is very obvious but sadly today's 911 has become short-nosed, too cab-forward and visually tail-heavy in side profile: classic 356 retains its equilibrium.

Above: The domed roof and 1950s modernism also hinted at 1930s aerodyne forms. This car has no excess, yet is not austere nor derivative device, it is an original masterpiece. Words fail to capture its essence, or the superb restoration of this particular 356.

Left: Single vent and super badges on the back of 411 YUH.

'DMY' was a perfect Roger Bray restoration (in 1991) and marks out this blue bird – originally supplied by AFN Porsche in the UK. Very few such cars were sold in right-hand drive and this one defines what a 356 cabriolet means. Note the exhaust venting from the rear over-riders in an act of applied design.

Chasing Porsches along country roads can be very rewarding. Seconds later she took off and flew.

Brilliance at Bicester: that sliver and blue-striped 356 keeps appearing.

Above left: Badges: another Porsche passion and these seen on a 356 are a superb story of an owner's enthusiasm.

Above right: Sculpture in steel: 356's floorpan was simple but effective.

Right: 'Ferry' Porsche (1909-1998) at the wheel of the car he oversaw in his father's absence and subsequent decline. This is Porsche personified.

First Porsches. Gmund and early testing,

Aerodynamic tuft testing on the move – on the road. Note how the airflow tuft-makers show mostly smooth flow over the car's flanks and turret. (*Photo: Porsche*)

Above: The roadster K45 286 of 1948 is the first true Porsche-branded car and on its far left edge, we see Erwin Komenda who joined Ferdinand Senior (seen right) in the 1930s and really was some form of co-founder of the Porsche design hallmark. A young 'Ferry' Porsche stands in the middle watching over the car he influenced so closely.

Left: The elegant lady sitting on a castle wall is seen with what we now call a 'Pre-A' 356 – but with cranked or bent, but not spilt, windscreen.

All is not what it seems with this Technics 550 'Spyder', but if it brings pleasure as an evocation, who are we to condemn its happy driver…

2

Luftgekühlt in Heaven

911 heaven – but in fact it is a wonderful 912. A pure, early car with all that means. Head off to see Max Levell at Revival Cars (near Heathrow Airport) if you want to fly a 912 – the sweet handling act of Porsche free-thinking – if your mind is open to it.

911 may be a magic number, but at its launch, the good burghers of 1963 into 1964 were somewhat shocked that their 356 pocket rocket had metamorphosed into something bigger, something more showy and of less overtly austerity-purist design language – but of course 911 was not flash nor showy nor bling, although you might think some of the more recent 911s are heading that way with over-sized gold wheels and obese hips, or you might not …

But air-cooled (*Luftgekühlt*) ruled, as did the 'flat' horizontal engine of low centre of gravity and great efficiency, but above all there was that sound, a sound that still entrances even the most rational of minds to evocation of its music.

Tuning a flat-six is an art. If, 300 years ago, the organ tuners of Bohemia were revered masters, so more recently, tuners of the Porsche flat-six are masters of their art.

The same channel goes with the engines. Jazz loving, piano-playing Hans Mezger (who would play Ella Fitzgerald on the stereo of his 911 Turbo as he drove) was the latter-day genius who became synonymous with the 911's flat-six engine and rightly so – we even have the phrase 'Mezger engine'. Yet he joined Porsche as early as 1956. But what of other members of the original team such as ex-Tatra engineer Leopold Janstche, or Helmuth Bott? What of Norbert Singer, Hans Tomola, and Klaus von Rucker? There are others. Whatever your view, they were the men of Porsche from 356 to 911 and in some cases, beyond.

Prior to the 911, there came the Porsche 904 GTS, this stunning body design by Butzi Porsche was perfect and timeless, but underneath the final twist of 356 and a Carrera engine were to be initially deployed. Although not technically a production road-going Porsche, this car cannot go unmentioned as it drew together many aspects of Porsche engineering and design and was sold in just over 100 examples. The exquisite 904 was a massive step forwards in design terms for Porsche and was styled by Butzi as he was creating the 'next-step' that was the 901 project – the 911 that we have come to adore.

Having a Porsche family member (Ferdinand Piech) on the engine team meant that the usual issue of cost and approval for the spending of it was made easier. Specifying quality and its cost was not a problem.

Of note, 911 continued the ellipsoid, teardrop form of the 356 but in a more modern context. Of interest was the elegant tail, the emotional or graphical shape of the front windscreen, and the hallmark sculpting of the front wings, bonnet (hood) and headlamps treatment – here was the new 'face' of Porsche.

Teardrop or ellipsoid shapes are not always as aerodynamic as you might think. The curves can create unwanted lift and also an ill-defined separation of the air as it falls or flows off the curved body. So much work was required to hone the 911's shape. The spectre of rear-end lift had to be dealt with and the ultimate demonstration of that became the famous 'ducktail' rear spoiler.

For 911, drag coefficient of CD 0.381 (corrected) was reliably cited in the Stuttgart University wind tunnel for the 911 in road-going 'owner' trim

including door mirrors and vertical number plate at the front. However the addition of extra trims, wider wheels and bodywork changes would worsen this figure, not improve it. The cross sectional frontal area CDS was a good figure of 0.642. However, wheel arch flares, wider tyres and new trims would increase this to a worse figure.

911's best recorded drag coefficient when fitted with rear spoiler, low drag door mirrors and re-profiling of certain under panels and the front air dam panel was cited at CD 0.363, which given its very upright front windscreen angle and guttering is exceptionally good

The early short wheelbase 1964 911s were perhaps the 'pure' representation of a smart but uncomplicated sports car. But some initial issues were soon obvious and continuous improvement began. A longer wheelbase did not detract from the formula.

Ventilated disc brakes would also soon be added for 1965. Early 911s used narrow 4.5inch width wheels; by 1966, 5.5inch wheels had been substituted. Improvements in the engine included new nitrided connecting rods and modified cylinder heads, valves and timing. Such were the first steps of what became a fifty-year development programme that became Porsche's 'continuous improvement'.

The 911 Targa model with its removable roof panel and roll bar hoop was the world's first mass production version of such a design feature.

But what of the flat-four-cylinder 912? That car turns-in with sensitivity; it picks up its skirts and clatters along very nicely and with 30mpg economy too. The suspension has less work to do because the car is lighter, and the ride is more compliant but has no under-damping nor wallow. 912 values are going up fast. There is a man in Germany named Kim Koehler at *Klassik Kontor* who loves 912s and he might be the champion of 912 to come. In fact, 912 and 912E values seem to be reaching 911 values – proof then that niche does not imply nonentity. Try American 912 experts, or Revival-Cars near London Heathrow Airport for solely 912-focused rescues and remedies. Andy Prill, the renowned Porsche expert, also began his journey with a 912 project – in case 911 purists do not know. So there is a lot of 912 love out there. Prill, by the way, having done so much with Lee Maxted-Page as Porsche specialist, latterly took over the Maxted-Page Porsche specialism legacy under a new Prill Porsche Classics banner.

Back with the 1970s, the 911 range-topper revived the 'Carrera' name previously seen on the 356. This 911 as the 1972 'RS' car, and was fitted with a 210bhp engine, mechanical fuel injection (the first deployment of the 'duck-tail' rear spoiler and also fitted with special 'Carrera' graphics down the sides of the car), and revised technical and trim specifications. That new RS rear spoiler was neither a styling tweak nor a marketing trick, instead it was a vital scientifically-proven addition. The new rear spoiler and revised integral front air dam worked to reduce the 911's aerodynamic lift at high speed – a reduction of over 60 per cent.

Driving an early 'pure' 911 provides an interesting experience in comparison to more recent 911s. You climb in to small cockpit and everything fell into place – notably those floor-mounted pedals. The steering wheel just seemed so right. The cabin was like a comfy little cockpit – not dissimilar to 356, but bigger, less austere and less upright. Once warmed up, the engine's clatter subsided a bit and you were off. This was direct, mechanical, visceral experience. Above a certain speed (about 60mph) the car's character changed and 911 seemed to pick itself up and enter a different yet unique driving experience. This car steered like a Supermarine Spitfire flew (Me Bf 109 not ignored!) –that is with telepathic feel and instant reactions, albeit the Spitfire did not have the 911's sting in its turning tail …

911 got sharper and harder in its RS, then 930 Turbo, 964 and 993 iterations, but always that special feel remained – one that stemmed from 356 then from 911. They just needed *driving*.

Right: F.A. 'Butzi' Porsche (1935-2012), the grandson of Porsche Senior, seen carving a 911 clay model into existence. (*Photo: Porsche*)

Below: Goodwood Members Meeting and a trio of early 911s burble and clatter their way to their moments. One is a 901-series, all are shorter wheelbase and utterly classic.

Above left: Classic noses: 1970s 911s front up in the three strongest colours of the era. But which blue is the front car – Adria Blue, Aga Blue, Arrow Blue, Mexico Blue, Oslo Blue? Or one of the other Porsche blues? It cannot be Riveria Blue as that came years later. Let's go with a fresh new Turqouise Blue from the Porsche paint card.

Above right: From the ellipsoid rear: blue 911, Blood Orange 911 and HMY 4K as a lovely 911 2.4S with rear-wiper and revised trim but it's not in Tangerine, so is it Signal Orange in one view or Signal Yellow in another?

Right: For 911S, Porsche simply black-coated everything, including the steering wheel. No chrome around the dials or on the wheel. No Houndstooth 'Pepita' Check on the seats but more black stuff.

Below: 911 Classicism as a 1966 car squats at the rear and noses up under power at the end of another great day at Bicester.

Above: Perfection of purist form. Note the orange car has sill plates and bumper trims to the moulded valances. Oh, and does 'Pepita' Houndstooth Check makes it 'pure'?

Right: Josh Sadler's more recent ride. The former RS of the President of the Porsche Club de France – with a lovely ducktail – *Entenbürzel* in German or *Queue de Canard* in French. The curve of those rear wings shouts '911'.

It's blue with Fuchs alloys and Porsche side-stripes. So it is lovely and it happens to be 912 which in the author's opinion makes it sweet and a step beyond the expected 911 narrative.

Classic collection tricolori. They just seethe, do they not?

RSR on the go: the Howells car turns in to Pardon Corner with obvious alacrity. The width of the rear wheel/tyre specification is obvious.

912 delight of US specification carousing through the Cotswolds. Note the hooded headlamps rings.

911 RS reflections: it is the classic angle. It sounds great too.

Seen from below and looking like a model, this is the real RS thing. An unusual view of a great car.

Seen from above in a view that captures the lobed form of 911; the late, thin-bumper 1973, ducktail-equipped, Carrera RS-decalled 911, has a curious 2.4 badge on its rump.

The form and function of 911 as static art. RGX is in the rare Bahia Red (*Bahiarot*), is it not?

Right: Only 33 genuine 911 ST cars were built as part of the development process in 1969-1970 and 'ST' was developed as a production specification pack rather than a car model. Josh Sadler the Porsche guru owned this original 1969 Porsche car which was a factory development car up to 1972 when a Porsche employee (named Ruf!) purchased it. Sadler rebuilt the car as a 2.3-litre with pure Porsche parts. More recently raced it at Rennsport reunion at Daytona. To confuse things, he sold the car, but the registration is now seen on Sadler's latest 1975-vintage 911 hill climb car.

Below: 911 in narrow-body form with Martini stripes. Stirred not shaken.

Above: This view is interesting because it allows the viewer to see just how much girth the new-generation 911 has put on in comparison to the pure early 911/912 bodyshell. AHJ looks small and delicate in comparison to the short-nosed Speed Yellow 'Bahn-stormer beside it.

Left: 912 scripted in gold. Lovely stuff in detail.

Above: A 912 looking all 'pointy' and up on its haunches ready to rock. Those podded extra lamps look great.

Right: RS 2.7 in Gulf Orange with arch extensions, wider wheels and two massive pipes out the back under the ducktail. There is a roll-cage in there too. Snick it down a gear and push!

This flat-six engine speaks its visual magic. Shame the fan drive belt is marked 'Made in PRC'! Not quite on old boy, really … Someone put a German one on for goodness' sake.

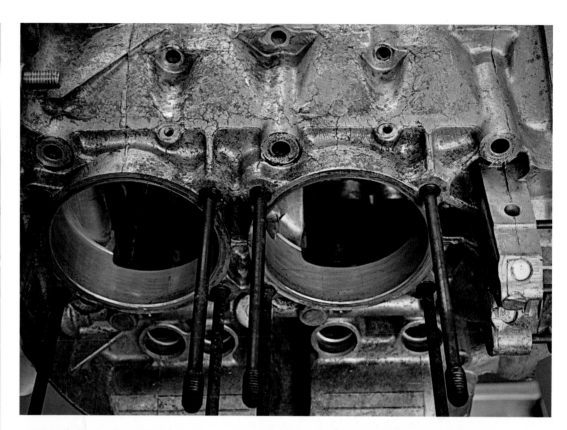

Above: Hans Mezger the hero. Porsche's engine guru beyond legend. A piano-playing, Jazz loving man of Swabia who used to play Ella Fitzgerald at full blast in his 911 Turbo as he drove. Mezger had a lifelong interest in art, music, and aviation, as well as his free-thinking engineering. His mind was German – and from 1956 Porsche-trained, but free of traditional rules of entrapment –which is how he did what he did.

Above right: Casting magic in the Porsche pots.

Right: Was this fan for the flat-six Tatra inspired via Porsche engineer Leopold Jantschke who had once worked for Tatra on Ledwinka's gems? Jantschke held a Porsche patent (German application number Cl. 12345.1 of April 2- 1951), and thence a U.S. and worldwide patent in 1952)from 1951/1952on a space-saving air-cooled, air-blower, two-cycle engine with a scavenging pumpfor car and tractor use, and he was latterly integral to 356 engine development. Mezger was integral to 911 engine development.

Through the Porsche porthole: flat-six moment.

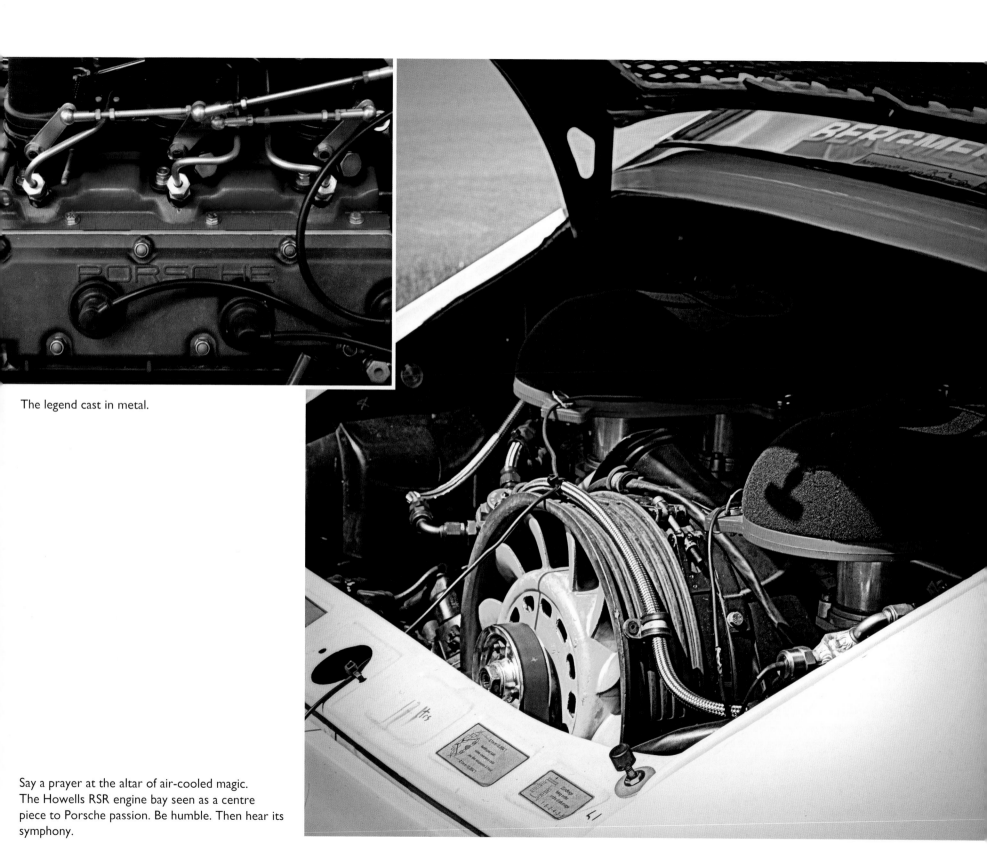

The legend cast in metal.

Say a prayer at the altar of air-cooled magic. The Howells RSR engine bay seen as a centre piece to Porsche passion. Be humble. Then hear its symphony.

964 RS engine bay looking all modern and shrouded in the Devil's plastic. Still, it went well, did it not?

3

On the Cam(s)

The author's Porsche passion extends to painting Porsches – like these 911s.

The first-ever 'Porsches at Prescott' in 2019 was a stunning evocation of the emotion of Porsche enthusiasm. I was there from the pre-event build-day to end of the two-day Porsche fest. Whatever the social or monetary differences of the attendees, the thing that mattered was the cars – the Porsches. Supported by Peter Lovett's Official Porsche Centre Tewksbury and by Porsche GB and Porsche Club GB, this was a significant new moment in the Porsche culture of Great Britain. People came from far and wide to sup at the grail of Prescott and of Porsches on the go amid a pits open to all with no VIP, self-entitled, or 'celeb' zones allowed.

Also seen in action were past-champion Paul Howells in his ex-Björn Waldegaard 2.8 RSR, and numerous tweaked 911s. Justin Mather's 924/944-engined car also drove well as always – he holds more than one Porsche club speed title. 911 guru (and Allard) fan, Josh Sadler turned up with his 911 'VRC' his (black not red) new Hill Climb car of interesting provenance and Porsche parts. Sadler has sold his rare 911S/T works development car.

The ex-Derek Bell/Stefan Bellof, 1982, Norbert Singer-built 956/07 Group C prototype arrived for static display at Prescott. Derek Bell is typical of the Porsche process and amid his many records and titles, we ought to just alight on the fact that Bell is the man who won Le Mans five times (four Porsche wins) and been podium-placed, all in Porsches 936, 956, 962C. Bell is the man who got 246mph on the Mulsanne Straight in the Porsche 917. His Bell/Bellof, Nurburgring, Porsche 956 is seen herein.

At the end of this great day of flashing colour and howling flat-sixes, my hair and my clothes were tainted with the smell and detritus of combustion and exhaust. But my mind was packed with images and memories of a wonderful new event in the calendar of Porsche.

Of ducktails and whale tails, of quad exhausts and airflow splitters, of screaming induction and singing exhausts, this was the Porsche culture up close and personal. Unlike certain other locations, Prescott has not gone 'VIP' or expensive. Anyone can enter for the cost of a few beers and a bottle of reasonable wine.

I must declare that I am member at Prescott, but receive no reward for promoting the brilliance of the place, its events, or Porsches at Prescott – which frankly is worth flying from afar to see, to smell, and to bathe in. The car park itself provided 911 heaven and beyond –over two days of passion.

What of Prescott Porsche people?

Try the PetroCanada Lubricants Porsche Club GB National Hill Climb Championship (with Pirelli support) rounds at Prescott (or Shelsley Walsh) to immerse yourself in the Porsche passion.

There, meet hillclimb champion and class leader, Robert Lancaster-Gaye who competes in his yellow road-going and hill-climbing 996 GT3 that, as described, he also drives on the road. He says it never goes wrong and has not suffered any 996 engine 'issues' – suggesting that maybe it is because the engine is driven as intended – hard but not without sensitivity and with plenty of warm-up and cool-down consideration prior to being stressed or turned off.

'Driving a 91 fast, with its rear-engine, has always been one of those big things,' says Robert. He equates it with other stimulating yet potentially risky pursuits. Given that he was the first Porsche Club Hill Climb Champion and has numerous other class wins to his name, we might assume that he knows what he is doing. He has driven Porsches competitively for twenty-five years and used ten different Porsches at Hill Climbs across that time.

Robert is a photography fan as well as passionate advocate of Porsche, so his car is the yellow 996 seen herein – howling along at speed.

Double title-holder Justin Mather is always open to a chat and can been seen fettling his 924S with its 2.7-litre 944 engine and 'interesting' glass fibre addenda – prior to yet another slingshot performance up a hill. Mather, like many Porsche drivers, is easy to approach and full of detailed Porsche dedication. Jonathan Williams and Laura Wardle have been campaigning a 911 Carrera at Prescott for three decades and are true 911 pilots.

Down at the Goodwood Members Meeting, a plethora of Porsches provided purism and passion under the focus of racing, high speed racing. Fancy seeing an ex-Elford car at full thrust? Goodwood Members Meeting is the place to saviour such memories. The accompanying photographs show what's on offer amid a wonderful gathering.

What it was to stand and stare at an ex-Vic Elford, 911 getting warmed up and ready for flight, or watch very early cars with great histories duck and dive and wail and sing through Goodwood's curves

You could hear the 911 names floating in the ether of history.

Vic Elford and co-driver David Stone won the 1967 Tour of Corsica in a 911R. The same pair won the 1967 Lyon-Charbonniere Rally in their 911. They also won the Tulip Rally and the Geneva Rally in 1967. Elford co-drove a 911 Sport-o-matic with J. Neerspach and H. Herrman to win the Marathon de la Route of 1967. Elford would win the 1968 Monte Carlo Rally, H. Toivonen would come second, both 911 mounted.

G. Larousse won the same race in a 911 in 1969 and won the Tour de France that year in a 911. A 91 won the 1967 Spa 24 Hours race at the hands of driver Gaban. B. Waldegaard won the 1969 Monte Carlo Rally in a 911S. Vic Elford and David Stone came second in their 911S. Hans Herrman took the 911 to the East African Safari as early as 1968 (911 won the 1968 World Rally Championship. The 911 was 2nd overall in the East African Rally of 1974.

In 1968, a 911 won the GT race at Watkins Glenn with Gregg and Everett driving. Gregg and Huth had won the GT race at the Nurburgring. Also in 1968, 911 triumphed in the GT class at Le Mans driven by Gaban and Schutz.

911 – notably as RSR 3.0-litre took ten national championship races in 1974 alone and the 1975 IMSA national Championship (USA) in 1975. John Fitzpatrick took the RSR to 1st in the GT class Le Mans 24 Hours in 1975. Le Mans would be where the heavily modified RSR 911s and 911 derivatives would perhaps be most visible. Who could forget Porsche's 800bhp 91 racer, the long-tailed 'Moby Dick' which made even the 935/936 and Kremer cars look tame. Derek Bell drove all manner of Porsches, including 911 derivatives, and remains a Porsche icon. Other 'names' of Porsche legend include Mass, Stuck, Wollek, Ickx, and Siffert. More recently, men like Peter Dumbreck have taken cars like the 997 GT3r to significant racing success. Josh Webster and Ben Barker are 911 Super Carrera Cup drivers of repute.

To this day, classic 911s, old and new, scream or howl up hill-climbs – even at decades-old tracks like Prescott. Silverstone and Goodwood events see 911s racing in all-out race competitions across the annual events calendar.

Josh Sadler is still hill-climbing his 911 and all these years on, Le Mans star Richard Attwood is *still* racing 911s –notably at Goodwoood.

Noted Porschepile Tony Dron achieved many successes driving various 911s across the pre-Millennium racing calendar. Nick Faure was a well-known 911 race-series driver and a Porsche dealer. Charles Ivey went 911 racing and the Ivey concern remain respected purveyors of 911s to this day. The Tuthill 911s are rightly admired as coming from a dedicated stable. Ex-Formula One drivers, right up to Mark Webber drive Porsche on the road and for races. From 1965 to date, Porsches, notably 911s, have been the choice of many champions.

From Shelsley to Silverstone, across the circuits and tracks, Porsches can be seen on the cam, hard at it, doing what they were designed to do. Therein lies the visceral experience of watching Porsches as well as driving them. The thing to do is simply stand and stare as history and Porsche passion meld into a moment never to be forgotten. And then there is that sound.

Ross McDonald goes through Pardon at Prescott in his 1979 3.0-litre which is hunkering down to let rip up the hill.

'Historika' indeed, via a December 1964-built 901-type car that made a big mark as one of the original batch of cars built by Porsche during the first three months of full 911 production. Andrew Jordan at the wheel at the 73rd Goodwood Members Meeting Aldington Trophy race. Narrow-body 911 heaven.

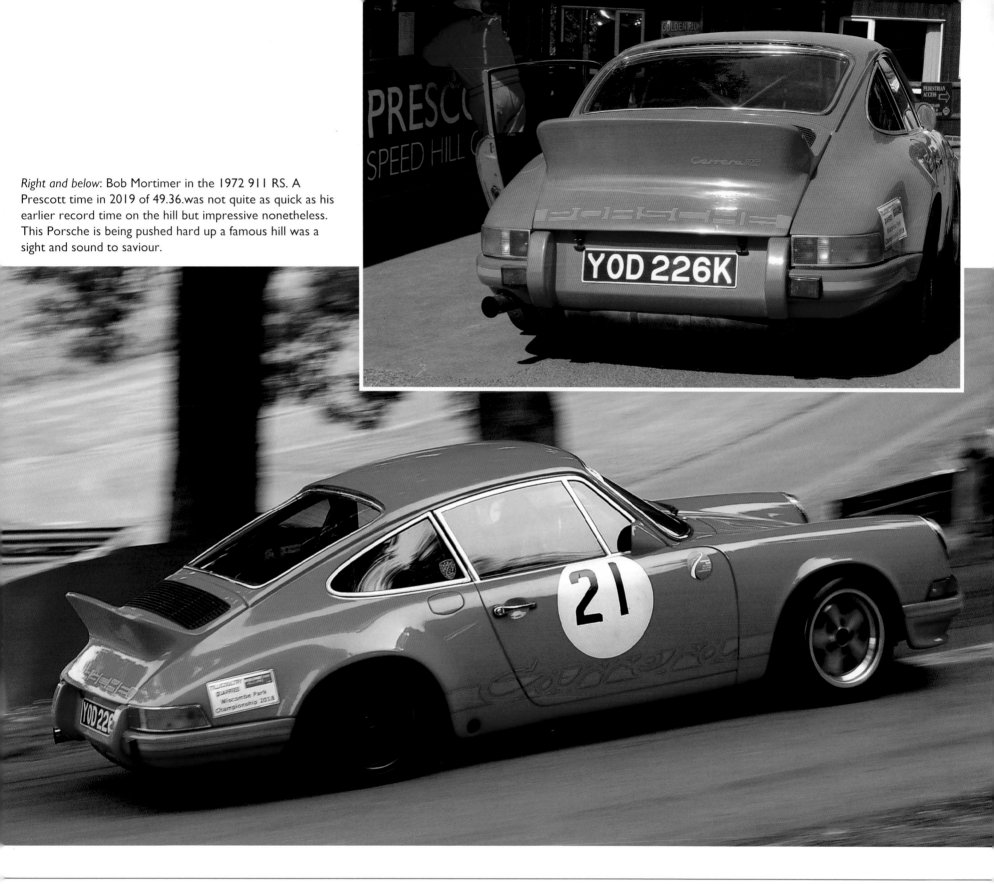

Right and below: Bob Mortimer in the 1972 911 RS. A Prescott time in 2019 of 49.36.was not quite as quick as his earlier record time on the hill but impressive nonetheless. This Porsche is being pushed hard up a famous hill was a sight and sound to saviour.

Porsche passion in the pits at Goodwood as the cars leave for the grid. People just stand and stare and listen. Phil Hindley leads Marshall Bailey for the off.

Two beautiful 911s turn in at Goodwood: timeless elegance. Simon Bowrey leads Peter Tognola.

Above left: The 959 in classic Rothmans livery. Gruppe B passion. (*Photo: Porsche/Author*)

Above right: Phil Price of Connaught Engineering campaigns this extended body 930-style 911 RS and all its Le Mans' type addenda. Get that rear wing. The downforce may be adequate.

Right: Marshall Bailey turns in tight at Goodwood in the pre-1966 911 Class of 2015.

Mark Bates of EB Motorsport hacks in as people watch Porsches. This car also raced at Spa in 2014.

Mark Leach at the wheel of an interesting 1972 3.0-litre i911 with lightweight fittings including Perspex (vented) rear side windows and 'Monza Record' 911 style front valance and indicator lenses, powers into Ettore's at Prescott.

Lee Maxted-Page of Maxted-Page the Porsche specialists (you know who they are) comes around the bend in an appropriately tagged car.

Bob Russell in the ex-Vic Elford 1965 911 gets the car warmed up properly – a vital issue for such a valuable engine. This was Porsche GB's 2.0-litre press fleet 911 in 1966 and hit 129.8mph at MIRA in 1966. Elford raced the car in 1967.

Bob Mortimer gets ready to at Prescott. He knows what he is doing, so relax.

911 cockpit before take-off. Five dials, roll-cage and that steering wheel – check. This is the stuff of 911 heaven. You should have heard it warming up …

Above: Well-known Porsche expert Peter Tognola (of Tognola Engineering) captured in classic repose as his January 1965-built 911, '901 TOG' seen at Goodwood Members 73rd Meeting as it turns-in with style. It has raced in the Old Timer Grand Prix at Nurburgring and is a Le Mans Classic veteran, not to mention at Silverstone and other surfaces.

Left: Chris Harris preparing to go at Goodwood in YRD 378C. 'Whang, whang,' went the flat-six a-warming.

Classic 911 sculptures at the ready. The magic of Goodwood Members Day 73rd meeting.

Josh Sadler, the 'Ducktail Druid' seen clambering out his recent 3.5 litre 911 modified hill-climb steed. He drove the 'twin-plug distributor'-equipped car to the event, competed, then drove it home! Sadler has now 'retired' from the specialist Porsche outfit Autofarm (he was its co-founder), but remains the guiding light of Porsche persuasion and after decades of excellence is the quietly spoken hero of a certain 911 movement. This was at Prescott in June 2021 in a blur of Porsche passion to take a class win against the young 'uns with a time of 49.31! Clearly there is no such thing as 'retirement'. The front-mounted oil-cooler was built by Lloyd Allard who is an expert at such exquisite jobs.

Wearing a 'VRC 911S' registration plate previously seen on Sadler's early 911 S/T development car, the ex-Bob Watson car now known as a 'Barn-find bitsa' spools up and Sadler presses the loud pedal and after a day's competition. The 46IDA Webers breathe and the car howls away in a blur of tuned and tweaked 3.5 litre air-cooled magic. The Group 4-spec rear spoiler screams 'PORSCHE'. Note the 16-inch wheels. Truly the song of the sirens.

This is the Howells 1973 RSR warming up in the Paddock at Prescott. Perspex adds lightness and those tyres add grip. Such cars are to savour.

Opposite: Essence of 911; up close in detail with the performance parts of the RSR.

RSR cruising with Howells at the wheel. Under power, unburnt combustion material exited the exhaust pipes out of Orchard. The sound was that unique air-cooled- oil-cooled boxer-engine harmonic that sound like a cross between a chainsaw and a prop-turbine jet spooling up .

Opposite: Snapshot of a siren; you know what sound it makes.

Above: Ross McDonald gets LRP ready as a new 991 GT3RS of Christian Ayres snarls at its ducktail.

Left: Laura Wardle retuned to Prescott in this the Williamson/Wardle 1972, 3.2-Litre car that has long been a regular competitor. There is something so special about an earlier, narrow-bodied 91 with a rear spoiler and side-stripes.

Above: It is the 'factory' 993 GT2 again – moving off in a rumble of raw purism. The names on the roof are Paul McLean and Peter Fairburn.

Right: 911 Safari is gaining profile as a specialist 911. This is the Porsche Museum car seen in unusual company at Goodwood.

The Bell/Bellof 956 as it arrived for Porsches at Prescott. Bow down in front of the King.

Above: Porsche/Norbert Singer engineering at rest with all the provenance and history of a great car.

Right: Take off the front panel and there is very little there – added lightness as the driver's tub is exposed.

Above: 911 fastbacks or as Porsche now wants you to call it, the 'Flyline'. Right …

Above left: 956: the wheel detail.

Left: Tails, fins, wings and things have always been a Porsche trademark mechanism.

Right: 997 4.0-Litre GT RSR with 480bhp then 450bhp at 7800rom (chassis #WP0ZZZ99Z9S99918) ran five times at Le Mans and is one of only twenty such cars built. Team Felbermayr, mit Blau – very evocative but those extended front wheel arches will play hell with the airflow. Two such Felbmermayr 997s were built one of 2007 and the other of 2009 basis. This is the 2009 car as driven by Horst Felbermayr Snr. and Jr., and Miroslav Konopka at Le Mans in 2010. Note the unique bonnet louvres.

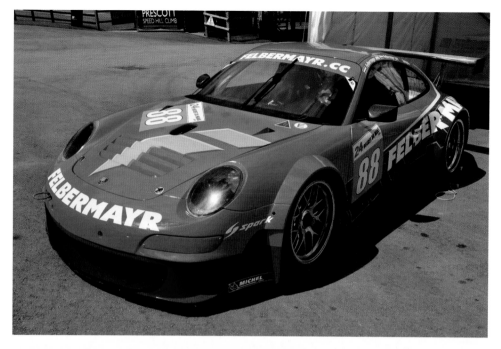

Below: An evocative gathering of Porsche racers gather in the English sun. 911s across the decades simply sit and make their timeless statement.

'Rose and Riley' have run two mixed-DNA 924/944 cars and this, the yellow car slithered around Prescott's Pardon Corner in 2021 as motor sport got back on its feet. Graham Rose at the helm of the lowered transaxle beastie making more Porsche passion of lateral thinking: great stuff.

Above: 911-964 as a Porsche Supercup competitor seen awaiting launch up the Goodwood hill. She burbled away with heat rising from the rear deck.

Right: Emanuele Pirro is a Le Mans victor several times over and raced this 911 GT3 Cup in the Porsche Supercup series. Here it is seen in all its Martini Racing livery looking as only a 'race' 911 can, whatever its era.

Left and below: Two views of a beautiful decaled but road-going 911 GT3RS in dark metallic blue with white and gold livery highlights. In 2014 this car ran in the Gumball 3000.

Above: New Porsches, old stripes. 911 atmosphere at the Porsche Cup.

Right: Porsche atmosphere. Robert Lancaster-Gaye's yellow 996 GT3 frames a resting helmet on a GT3RS rear wing.

4

Newer Neunelfer

This sunroof-equipped 964 is rarer in its blue hue. As you can see, the occupants are enjoying the ride. Driving in its finest form – to quote a Porsche statement of old.

Of the 959? This concept car that become production reality was a big step and a gateway to a new era of Weissach and Porsche. Conceived at the height of the Group B racing specification era, 959 capitalised on such investment in that potential by creating a new Porsche 'technology' hallmark for the mid-1980s – bridging the step into a new era of automotive engineering. Ultimately, 959 was a technology showcase for what Porsche could do. Basing it around an old, but much-modified 911 shell seemed odd, but saved huge amounts of money in terms of body engineering and tooling.

The man behind the 959 as 'Project B' was Helmuth Bott – Porsche's great engineer of the 911 era. The man who led the engineering development of the car was Manfred Bantle. Anatole Lapine and his team created the styling. Roland Kussmaul was 959's lead development engineer.

Unveiled at the 1983 Frankfurt Motor Show, as a concept 'one off' the 911 Gruppe B, was a 400bhp prototype that caused quite a stir. But it was not called 959 at this stage and few suspected that it would become a production-series Porsche.

If 959 had made limited mark upon the consciousness of car design, and marks upon motorsport via the Paris – Dakar and at Le Mans, the wider production availability of the 'new' 911 that was the 964, touched a wider customer and enthusiast base.

The 964 RS rather proved the point that Porsche could still develop the 911 formula, but 964 had tamed a bit of the 911's wayward character. But as the 3.6-litre Carrera 2, 964 reached satisfying heights for all but the on-road racing driver. Removing the four wheel-drive and improving the steering and gearbox had added some reverse-engineered character.

964 – being almost all new was also built in a new way with many new efficiencies over how the old car was constructed. Thoroughly modernised, 964 was better, stronger, safer, had revised engines, suspension, drivetrain and structure, yet it looked like an older 911 and even used the same glass for its windows and windscreens.

964 was brilliant and brought in four wheel-drive, with a viscous coupling controlled, Ferguson-type epicyclic central transmission differential which directed 31 per cent of the torque to the front wheel and 69 per cent to the rear. 964 C4 gave 911 new handling – at the cost of a touch of steering telepathy – and ultimately there was 964RS. Initially launched with four-wheel drive, latterly with two-wheel drive (and better for it said some) 964 changed the character of the 911, it was more refined and less pure and, even in Turbo form, less raw.

But 964 looked very familiar – too familiar for some, but familiar enough for others – the purists. Yet as a 360bhp, 3.6-litre Turbo 3.6 with a top speed that could nudge 180mph, 964 reached new 911 heights. Key variants included the Carrera 4 and Carrera 2, and when did you last see a 964 Targa? They existed, but in low numbers, as did the flat-nose of 'Flachbau' series cars.

For some people, 964 is the jumping-off point for a tranche of Porsche purism. Fair enough. But afterwards came the next step as the 991 as 993-series which added major design and body changes to the 911 and 964 underpinnings hidden below its new Tony Hatter- styled sculpture amid design chief Lagaay's suggested substantial visual changes to the body of the 911 which led to 993.

993 delivered innovation and Porsche's first six-speed manual gearbox (Type G50/21). In 993, Porsche ended its semi-trailing arm rear suspension and created a contemporary multi-link set up. The car also introduced 'VarioRam' variable intake timing and induction system in 1996.

993's remit was to be safer, more aerodynamic, easier to make and as such was perhaps the first true reinterpretation of 911. Improving on the old 911 bodyshell's old-fashioned tolerance was not easy, major re-engineering above even that of the 964's being required. 993 resembled the Porsche 959 hyper car and had a new style that was of significant effect on 911's legend. But some 911 lovers felt and still feel that 993 was a step-too far. But people said that about the new 911 in 1964 when it replaced the 356!

The 993 Turbo with four-wheel drive and top speed of over 180mph proved a point and so too did the ultimate road-racers as RSR, and as GT1, GT2, and later contexts of 'GT' series 911s. Of note was the 993 GT2/RS of 1995-1998 with two-wheel drive, bi-plane rear spoiler and riveted arch extensions. Add in some RUF parts and you had an outlaw 993.

993 also created a completely new Targa model with a clever glass roof that slid backwards and downwards – taking its cue from the very clever 1989 Panamericana concept car designed by Steve Murkett.

After 993 came huge change and much controversy. We must surely see that the old 911 not even amid its 964 and 993-series could go on unchanged for ever.

Porsche's management took the decision to develop a new two-seat soft-top (the Boxster) and a totally new 911. Both cars would share just over 30 per cent of their parts and be almost identical in structural and under-the-skin tooling from the B-pillars forwards to the nose. This 'shared commonality' 911 was to be called the 996 series. 996 would step away from air-cooling and use a water-cooled M96 engine – but still a flat-six. So began the arguments. But today 996 is maturing nicely and proving its point, not least in GT3 RS form.

Yet in the new 996, much was changed. But the water-cooled, organically-styled 996 earned money and helped keep Porsche going at time of global market downturn and a narrowing of Porsche's market offering: 996 earned new customers and no one should ever forget that 996 seems to be rust resistant too. Despite its water cooling, 996 sounded like a Porsche, drove like a 911 should and was stronger and safer than ever – not least as 996 was 45 per cent stiffer than its predecessors in torsional rigidity.

996 is not everyone's favourite Porsche but today we can look at it, notably in MkII or 'Gen 2' variant and see that it was and remains a good car and one that contained much of Porsche. 996 remains accessible in pricing terms for its lower models and allows many enthusiasts access to Porsche ownership at reasonable price. Only those living in their own exalted bubble would dismiss such opportunity for people of less than 'high net worth'.

Yes, 996 was a different take on the 911, but hasn't it come into its own now? You may of course completely disagree. Speaking personally, operating on limited funds, I would rather use a well-serviced 996 as my daily-driver as opposed to spending the same amount to purchase a domestic appliance that masquerades as a motor car and is about as inspiring as a sadly flattened hedgehog.

After 996, Porsche presented the 997 as a step forwards and a step backwards to more traditional 911 design language. Was 997 the last of the smaller, nimble, narrower, 911s in a modern context? Water-cooled, yet with mechanical steering and all the usual Porsche ingredients, the 997 model range echoed the 911 DNA.

997 became full-fledged as Turbo, Carrera, S, GT2 / Lightweight, GT3, and GT3RS variations – right up towards 500bhp and 200mph performance. Porsche had recaptured the essence of the 911 story in the 997 as far as was possible and in 3.8-litre Carrera S, GT3 and GT3RS forms, and finally in the rare, 4.0-litre GT: all received many superlatives from drivers and owners. 997 also became a Speedster model in the true sense of all that name meant.

Clearly, 997 was a great development and became a very useable 911 prior to its widening into 991-series where even the 'basic' 911 came with over 300bhp. 991 and 992 took 911 beyond its past into a new technology, into detailed design yet amid an image of massive wheels and even wider rear wing hips in a digital reincarnation of 911.

We can divide the 911 story into the distinct eras that encompass the 1960s, 1980s, and beyond the Millennium to date. The latest 992 is brilliant, but far removed from the character of its genesis. For 911 is now a much larger car than its early ancestors, yet it remains probably the most desired sports car in the marketplace. Some purists may feel that it has changed too far, but others might say it has simply evolved and moved with the times. For some, 911 is Porsche, solely. But in fairness, we really must see beyond the 911 bubble to a wider Porsche horizon. As usual, you are free to disagree and retreat into your fortress 911 heaven.

A subtle 930-series turbo shows off its wide-bodied form and classic-era class.

This is an 'RSR' body and very rare — but is on a based on a 1975 911. It is suitably mechanically modified and evokes all it should. Note the front bumper valance cooler inlet and the vents in the wide-body rear wings. The car is heading a trio of tuned-up 911s as they glide into Greatworth Classics Porsche day. If you want to be pompous about recreations, that is your affair.

This late Targa looks fantastic in metallic gold and later-spec wheels. The paint looks like the alluring Gazelle Metallic (#406) from 1974-75 but the car looks later. 187 Targas were built in Gazelle Metallic and 275 Coupé Turbos likewise. Sand Beige or Gold metallic anyone?

Above: For some, this seat trim is the thing to have, others hate it. Known as 'Pasha' (or Chequerboard or *Schachbrett* mimicking a motor racing flag) it emerged from Lapine's studio in 1977 under 'Op Art' *a la mode* and was seen on 911s (notably the SC specification) and of note the launch 928. Some say it was inspired by a butterfly's wing pattern. Whichever version is true, this example is in Navy with contrasting panels – very smart. Only Hans Michel Piech's 'Paisley' pattern special interior for his 1973 Carrera RS 2.7 was more visually confusing. What of Tartan seats in a Porsche – thank Louise Piech for that.

Left: This mid-1980s 911 has been re-worked as a brilliant modified car with a later 964 engine transplant and many technical upgrades by its owner Alex. The blue hue is just so 911. Those exhausts set into the rear valance once exited from a 14in Magnaflow box but further work and heat exchanger mods saw some 993-specification tubes and bits which sorted out the tube bore and the breathing apparently. The wheels and suspension also lend an air of 'outlaw' thinking. No gold wheels here thank goodness. Just don't rush the gearchanges with the 915's box …

More modification magic; low-drag mirror, 993 GT-type rear wing, extended arches, bonnet catches, Fuchs wheels,

Narrow-body classic 911 of the great SC into Carrera 2 era of the early 1980s when 3.0-litres became 3.2-litres of Porsche push. The last iteration of 'early' 911 prior to the 964 arrived.

Above and opposite: Another 911 *modificato* as an 'RSR' of 1975 911 origins evokes Carrera RSR style. Gold wheels go with white ok so let's forgive them. The lip of the rear wing is at an interesting angle for airflow and wake vortex tuning.

Above: Butzi Porsche in his studio holding a scale model of his favourite Porsche design – the 904. There is a Dachshund sculpture on the window sill! (*Photo: Porsche*)

Right: Flat-six mindfulness; just stare.

D is for *Delphigrunmetallic* and was a 914 colour in the first instance, latterly applied at the factory to a very few 911 – including just one 911 Targa in 1974. Suitably, DAB 911S was captured amid fading light as she scythed along by sunset. The colour is that very rare 911 hue Delphi Green yet looks gold in this light. She is the development car for Classic Retrofit – where lead engineer Johnny Hart conjures up very clever upgrades to electrical and other systems. DAB now has two air condensers fitted up front and proper tropical zone air con. The front oil cooler has been cleverly re-engineered to the back end, so no oil lines front-to-rear because oil system moved rearwards. It is now up inside the rear quarter arch panel with its own fan and thermostat set at around 80 degrees. It needs less oil quantity (due to the shorter systems)and warms up more quickly yet stays cooler than standard. DAB also has better fuse box system, the exhaust has race headers with no heat exchangers and of note, an improved quality coil fitted giving 40 volts at the spark plug as opposed to the standard 30-ish. This car evidences the Porsche subculture and the fact that improvements do not always have to be at the expensive of design purity. Even Alois Ruf has had a look at DAB. Enough said.

This is a 1989 911 with classy backdating. Note the mirrors and the ducktail. It is retro but not pastiche. How very charming GXI 26 is.

Flying 964. Guards red caught on the go in the rain. *Whaaang* … pure Porsche sound on the cams.

Above left: 964 RS in a monochrome moment. Classic stuff indeed.

Above right: The Christian Ayre's 964 RS seen in all its colour – love it or loathe it, that colour of Rubystone is defining of a Porsche moment.

Right: As it left Stuttgart; just stare and say little.

Above: The Stone family 911 howls up hill in Gulf Blue and Orange. A nice prod on the power and she should revolve quite nicely.

Left and opposite above: 993 with RS kit and full GT-RSR 'bookshelf' rear wing. Oh the joy of 993 things. To the author, this is near the top of the 911 heaven tree. Note the 'critical separation-point' lip-spoiler at the top of the rear window to better control airflow down the rear end and onto that wing.

Right: Five chrome-dials and a Tiptronic shifter.

Above and opposite: Tony Hatter's 993 restyle of the 911 was a masterpiece of reinventing class. Here in these detail shots, we capture the essence of the scaled sculpture he created.

Above: Hatter's rear-end of 993 is timeless and shouts 'Porsche' at you in the subtlest of voices. The conflicting demands of cooling-in, venting-out, lift-reduction, and drag wake reduction off the back of the 993 led to hours of wind tunnel work to shape this wonderfully carved rear wing plate. Note the complex side plates and air funnels. An airflow triggerlip can be seen atop the rear screen to tune the boundary layer and airflow separation downwards over the rear windscreen ahead of the crucial main rear spoiler.

Opposite: Classic portrait of a classic car.

Above: When did you last see an orange 933? Deep hued joy.

Left: Suddenly, those controversial 996 headlamps look so right. It has taken time, but Pinky Lai's so-called disruptive design now seems so balanced and fresh. Maybe it took an outsider to re-invent the impossible? Unlike more recent 911s, 996 is not too short-nosed either. Lai deserves more credit for his achievement. Send the man some love.

Above: 996 with the correct 'Aero Cup' GT-series fittings in Speed Yellow. How very classic.

Right: Robert Lancaster-Gaye in his 996 GT3 careers up Prescott in blaze of Porscheism. This utterly reliable car competes at national level and takes its driver to some very competitive placings, not least winning the 2015 Porsche Club GB Hillclimb Championship. Robert encapsulates what the Porsche movement is about —people, cars and sheer open-minded enthusiasm.

997 GT RS 4.0-Litre. The collector's dream of a modern classic before the 911 grew fat. This one is being driven as intended .

Above: POR 911X looks rather retro-lovely in black; nice wheels. Steve Andrews cutting along in his 911 in the Cotswolds. Somehow, a black 911 (of any age) and without shiny window trims still looks very devilish indeed.

Right: Porsche GB press car as Riviera Blue with the full GT-spec. '911 GB' is a famous Porsche GB number plate but Riviera is just stunning in the shadows.

Carrera S moment; it's raining and the road is greasy, but the Porsche is punting along as intended. Seen in a more basic, less-adorned form, this 991 was the business.

Silver dream machine of a 997 G2 on the go. Was this the last stylistic link to the original 911 before the design became digital, short-nosed and fat-hipped? Some may think so.

How far do you want to go with Martini livery and applied patination? Still, it is free-thinking in a world of 911 rules, for which we could be thankful.

Above: Simon Tarling can be seen concentrating hard as he pushes the blue 996 Gen 2 hard up a hill. Blue is the Porsche wavelength to be on.

Opposite above: Melvin Spear (Porsche Club 964RS Register Secretary) in his well-known and rare 1991, 964 Carrera Cup type, chassis WP0ZZZ96ZM5409111: a car with a significant race history. Engineered by Porsche race engineer Roland Kussmaul, the Weissach-built 964 Cup/Super Cup-series were lighter and faster. At just over 1,100kg and with up to 305bhp on tap from the 2.6 litre M64 engine, the rear wheel-drive Carrera Cup cars respond with essential Porsche verve.

Opposite below: Peter Turnbull careers around Pardon in typically elegant fashion. The 997 GT-series looking lithe and 'pointy' on its rims.

GT3RS is all about the details.

Inside the GT3RS with swathes of the synthetic stuff and full seat harnesses. Hold on tight.

Above: P900 SPY is a well-known registration and has been seen on several of its owner's 911s. Here a yellow GT3 cruises by looking far too serene. But it is definitely a design classic.

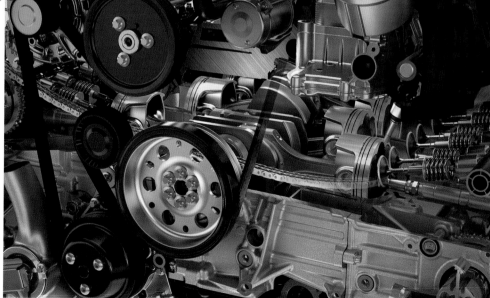

Right: Inside the heart of the 'Boxer' flat-six. It will not eb the same when the 911 goes in for electrickery. (*Photo: Porsche*)

991 Carrera T rests as storm brews up. Nice, but it's all about the haunches now, is it not?

Right: That rear end 'fly-line' as Porsche now want to call it still captures the essence of 911.

Below: Seen from this angle, the 991 looks longer nosed because the bumper prow is prominent. GT Silver looks good and the seat belts match the brake callipers. She is about squat and launch.

Reflections upon dedicated design. Only Porsche would go this much trouble with a headlamp design.

5

A Wider View

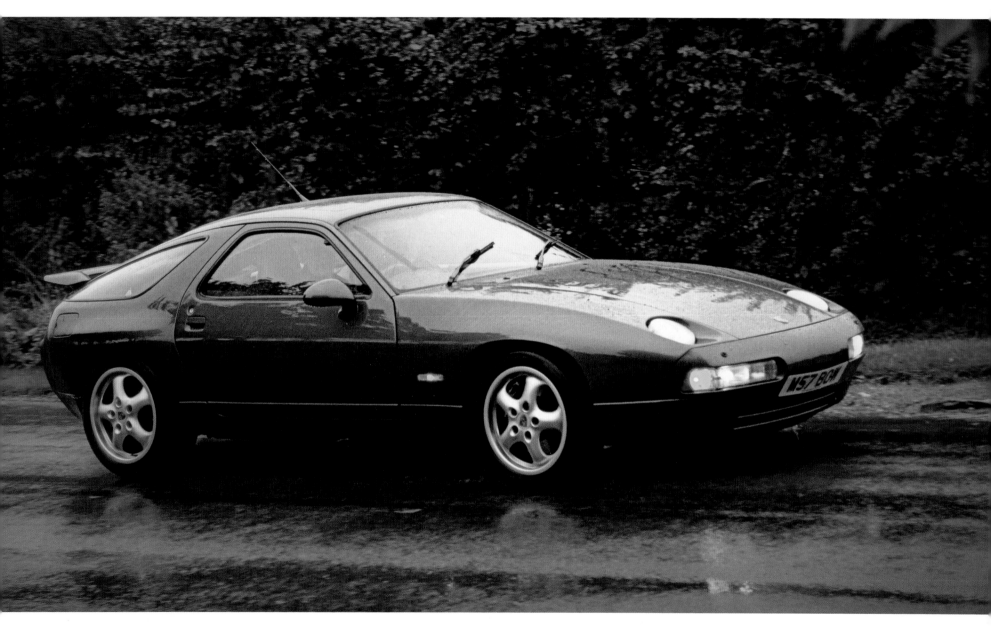

Subject to a negative narrative by some purists for years, 928 has won many friends over the decades for its colossal integrity of engineering and design. This GTS is cantering along in the rain and looking decidedly biomorphic in its ellipsoid elegance. Interest in the GTS remains strong worldwide – a manual gearbox being the key, but automatics were built. Just fifty one right-hand drive GTS were built, forty six of which came to the UK.

Porsche people can be harsh at time. Why else were so many 912s lost at the altar of 911 repair and restoration? Why was there such dismissal of this flat-four model over the flat-six champion? Why was the world-leading technology and design of the 928 sneered at so unfairly? Why was the 914 ignored and decried when in fact it encompassed many pure Porsche ingredients of design and driving? Why do people dismiss the 924 as having a van-engine when it did not?

These questions and others lie scattered across the landscape of the Porsche persuasion and many debates.

Of significance, it was Porsche 'purist' engineer Ernst Fuhrmann who took the very brave managerial decision to renounce the rear-engined air-cooled Porsche rule book. The man who was an essential part of the 356 and 911 story, Professor Ernst Fuhrmann, who was brought back into run Porsche from 1972 to 1980, prompted the concept of the water-cooled and front-engined new Porsches of 924, 944, and the 928: Fuhrmann (who so cleverly initiated Porsche's 1970s development of its Weissach engineering centre) challenged the unwritten law that a true or proper Porsche had, by some form of divine right or rule, to be air-cooled and above all, rear-engined. Hopefully, we have, by now, agreed with old Ernst, even if it is only up to a point.

914 was a project that helped widen Porsche's profile, not least in America, and was a car that won new 'conquest' customers who thought that they could not afford a Porsche and were perhaps wary of the 911s allure and legend.

For a car designed in the late-1960s to early-1970s, the 914 was a remarkably futuristic and 'clean' design of significant character. Compare it to mainstream car design of its era and 914's futurism shines. Various claims to the styling's origin lie in the 914's story but the initial body design is stated by many writers to have been originally out-sourced to a Swabian design bureau, Gugelot Design, and that they designed the car or at least created a prototype exercise. Gugelot were interested in synthetic plastic and resin moulding to achieve new shapes and had research links to Bayer's new synthetic resins plastics. However, Gugelot's original designs were according to some versions of the tale, possibly the inspiration for the 914's design rather than its final shape.

Did Gugelot's design become of influence but then become amended by Porsche for the 914 with Porsche design bureau and Butzi Porsche influence Other versions of the story say that the 914 was by a Porsche design engineer named Heinrich Klie. Klie, who had been at Porsche since he was the 356's clay modeller, worked for Butzi so some degree of cross-co-operation was likely. Michael von Klodt's forensic work in his book *Das Grosse VW-Porsche Buch*, also evidences that 914 was an in-house work of Porsche provenance and that Klie's design proposal won out over several other proposals. So even the little 914 was subject to design argument – as so many cars are.

914 began when Ferry Porsche and VW's Heinrich Nordoff (Nordoff's daughter had married a Piech family member) knew each other and shook hands on the kind of joint deal to develop a platform and 'shared' car that is now commonplace. The outcome was the 914 and then 914/6 amid a joint VW-Porsche marketing and sales branding exercise in Europe, yet as a Porsche in America – although VW-Porsche soon became a tag Stateside. Nordoff died before the car saw the road but his legacy lived on.

A new 1.7-litre four-pot VW engine gave it adequate performance amid excellent mid-engined handling, but the placement of the Porsche flat-six in the 914 created a rather more effective device. Given its lightweight, 940kg and over 100bhp, the 914/6 had performance gain that meant it could threaten the 911 on the race track or the road; an unintended consequence perhaps?

On sale from 1969 to 1975, the 914 four-pot sold 115, 631 units bit suffered from high build costs and a consequent high sales price.

Sadly denigrated, 914 was ignored for years – despite being voted America's 'Import' car of the year for 1970. The 914/6 sold just 3,338 units up to late 1972. Denied by Porsche purists for years, 914 and 914/6 can now surely be appreciated as 'pure' in their Porsche ethos and stunning design language inside and out. Few cars of its era were this well shaped or detailed.

Remember, 914 was mid-engined, a superb drive, strong, comfortable, stylish and had a Targa-top. Yes, they rusted more than they should have (from the inside-out) but 914 was much better than urban myth stated. In 914/6 GT trim the car became more muscular and it competed in major national class races and had a class win at Le Mans and podium places at Nurburgring in 1970. 914 was also the FIA's first-ever Formula One, event circuit 'Safety Car' – which was worth a lot of money as visible PR.

914 was short-lived but its VW four-cylinder engine briefly reappeared in the US market 912 E in 1975-1976.

Over five decades on, the little 914 and its six-pot offshoot, are now seen in a kinder light. They certainly are a great drive, being direct, informative, sprightly, and well-balanced and mannered – just like a Porsche should be.

The Porsche Club GB 914 Register provides a valuable resource for the cars and 914 registrar Kevin Clarke's 914/6 is seen at the front this book. He has owned twelve of the cars and currently has six. Kevin now quite correctly revels in the new profile of the car that he has always believed in.

You might not be a 914 fan, but be sure of one thing – it *was* part of the Porsche Process.

The next new generation Porsche was to be the 924 and it was built upon the idea of an 'entry-level' Porsche that the 912 and the 914 had leveraged respectively. Often stated to have a 'van' engine in 2.0-litre form, this is incorrect. It is simply that the VW-Audi engine design had been used in the stunning Audi 100 Coupe, then the 1977 Audi 100 Mk2 saloon; the engine was re-purposed for subsequent use in a VW van. But this did not a van-engine make it.

By way of a Porsche-VW agreement, it found its pre-paid-for way into the new 924 using an injected and modified version of the Audi 100 engine, which itself had been given a single-overhead-camshaft and enlarged bore during its own lifetime. A new injection system was a Bosch-Porsche design in the first place. Also added was a new alloy-built, cross-flow head on the old Audi engine's cast iron block. A new camshaft, main bearings, and oil pump and sump were also added. Only the belt-driven cam-drive came off the original Audi unit – that had also appeared in the VW LT van.

The 924's transaxle gearbox was also a new item as part of a comprehensively revised engineering package. Who invented the transaxle in 1929 – Ferdinand Porsche Snr!

A young Harm Lagaay's design for what became the 924 was almost complete at early attempt and beat two different (transaxle) proposals from Dawson Sellar and from Richard Soderberg. Interestingly, a little-known fact is that the large glass rear 'bubble' of the 924 reputedly stemmed from an aspect of Soderberg's design. As Lagaay said in Porsche press material, 'I was a young designer, just twenty five years old and I had a major hand in the 924.'

Lagaay had actually got most of the 924 right first time from his early sketches and it was more his design than anyone else's. Only some details were modified by his peers. He has also been keen to point out that although a VW project in its origination, 924 was designed at Porsche by Porsche for VW as a VW – so when Porsche took it back in-house, they were not buying a VW design, they were buying a VW designed by Porsche's design team in the first place. This is a major point that many 924 detractors have forgotten.

Amid the success of Porsche's 924 Carrera GT motor sport series, with the car taking places at Le Mans and a subsequent Carrera GTR series, Porsche did not ignore the marketing possibilities, hence the homologation special that was the 150mph 924 Carrera GT – a racing car turned into a road car of supreme ability.

Consider the 924 Carrera GT, then throw in the later 2.5-litre balance-shaft engine models and 924 begins to make its mark of Porsche and its 'ism'.

Today, the petite and nimble, great to drive, narrow-bodied 924, notably in Turbo and 2.5-litre guise, is a worthy addition to the Porsche enthusiasm and perhaps only a closed mind would call it not a 'proper' Porsche. But

therein lies the passion, the debate and the differences. It is why 911 stands alone – even if it would have never have been without 356.

The point of the 924-into-944 exercise was to move Porsche the brand further away from the VW-Audi origins of the 924, which even in Turbo guise, remained to many, a different strain of the Porsche DNA. Enter the 944 in which Porsche threw money at a new engine and at revamping the 924 to produce a 'new' car rather than facelift of an old car with a new body skin and little else – that would have failed. Aspects of the 928's engine design were to be found in this new 2.5-litre – which also found its way into the 924 and created a delightful little A and B road weapon of a car.

944 was good for just over 135mph/220kmh and managed the crucial 0-60mph/96kmh in a strong 7.2 seconds. The critical 50-70mph overtaking manoeuvre via a third gear that would run to 85mph/137kmh was also well inside the performance car norms at under eight seconds – the over-square engine's big cylinders, hefty crank and high torque really delivering, yet doing so with unusual response and lightness.

944 went on to become the 944 Turbo and also on to sixteen valve technology and of course as a racer and road-going racer as the GT, and as the restyled 968 as Clubsport variant. 968 was a redefined 944 engineering package (also with new gearbox options). Of note, 968's heavily revised engine used the early Porsche patented 'VariCam' mechanical auto-adjusting valve-timing refinement acting via the cam-chain altering the degrees of actuation to the inlet camshaft by up to 15° thus changing ignition advance at higher engine revolutions.

With its 928-style nose and 964-style details, it looked wonderful but was perhaps too late in the cycle to gain the appreciation it deserved.

Porsche threw everything at the 928, it did not just design a new car it created a new type of car. Professor Fuhrmann and Porsche took a huge gamble in the 1970s to agree to such a new type of car and to fund it. It is suggested he saw it as post-911 car for Porsche, but did he necessarily see it as a 911 replacement? That argument had raged for years amongst Porschephiles.

Contrary to some opinions, the 928 was never conceived to replace the 911, but to become the new definition of Porsche when the 911, as it was then framed, finally died – which most people assumed would be by the 1980s. Surely Porsche knew that a 'new' iteration of Porsche's ethos and character was needed if Porsche was to survive beyond its family enclave and 911 cocoon? Could a soul be recast?

928 was new thinking, new technology taken to the exquisite, at huge cost, yet often lumped in with more normal competitor vehicles in road test and comparisons. These were traditionally engineered cars whereas 928 was new technology: 928 deployed the 'Weissach'-type wishbone rear axle

with multi-link mountings and a self-adjusting angle-mode compensator to adjust the rear wheels behaviours.

Wolfgang Eyb was the chief engineer of the 928 and his forensic skills further honed the car – his 928 project manager W. Gorissen led a team of engineers and designers who had the vision to create massive change and something more – a next step design. Under Lapine's direction, Wolfgang Mobius was the lead body design stylist and Dawson Sellar created the interior design.

Inspired by Prof Furhmann's own, turbocharged 928, a more powerful, non-turbo bhp increase was ordered. The late-1979 launched revision known as the 928S saw an increase in power by 25 per cent via increased bore and stroke to 4,664 cc, 305bhp/225kW and a 10:1 compression ratio. Deleting the cylinder liners increased combustion volume. Fuel injection changes were also made.

Then came the further S-series variants and then stunning GTS – a harder 928. The difference between the 928 at launch in 1979 and the 928 GTS 1992 was transformative. The 928 GTS of 1992 replaced all previous 928s and delivered 350bhp, and a 5.4-litre engine.

The GTS could lope along the motorway, but press the throttle into the carpet and it stormed away like a crack of thunder – nose up, rear squatting, quad-cam singing, GTS was fast and somehow more raw. This was a performance car that was quicker than a 911 3.3-litre Turbo and showing it a long sweeping bend or tight S-bend revealed wonderfully balanced handling and poise: if the back end did finally shift on you, a good dab of opposite lock and neutral (not extreme lift-off) power soon had it slithering away.

Only fifty-one right hand drive GTS manuals were built, and forty four arrived in Porsche GB's hallowed halls for distribution to dealers. Leaner, meaner and now more valuable, as a GTS 928 evolved into a classic Porsche.

So changed Porsche across the years – yet 911 continues as the icon. We must assume that there will be resistance to an all-electric 911 for some time to come. After all, if that is what you want, buy a Taycan.

Meanwhile, beyond the great big Porsche branding machine, there lie the specials, the outlaws and the enthusiasts of Porsche subculture. Be it RUF, FVD Brombacher, Emory, Singer, Restoration Design, Design 911, or anyone you care to mention from the long list of dedicated Porsche providers, this Porsche culture has bred many offshoots, many legacies and many moments of pure joy for the people that populate it and the Porsches that they drive and love.

Long may they (and the Porsche AG big brand itself) prosper as providers of that thing that men and women desire – a drivers' car of advanced or different design. For Porsche is a passion, and just in case your purist mind forgot, it is one that starts before 911 and goes beyond that car, while all the time, respecting and referring to 911 and more. It really is a case of 911 heaven *and* beyond…

Opposite: the later rear infill panel is a love it or hate it addition to 928 originality, but GTS did get a rear wing that actually performed an aerodynamic function. GTS has a following in Australia and in America.

Donald Peach's lovely 928S is pure class in its colour and trim combination. The clever curves of Wolfgang Möbius styling remains timeless beyond fashion.

Above: 'EWV' is a well-known 914 four-cylinder and captures the essence of the 914's great design. Unadorned, scaled, sculpted and unlike any other car, 914 was a great piece of industrial design –albeit one undermined by a narrative and, a regretful passion for rust. The 'Porsche' script across the rear bulkhead was design purity of great subtlety. We should thank Ferry Porsche and Heinrich Nordhoff for being brave enough to create the 914 project.

Right: Porsche passion is about people as well as cars. Here, 914 displays its stunning design elements and as you can see, 914 provides huge fun and access to the Porsche process. It's about driving, not a damned corporate-speak 'ownership experience'. Porsche took the 914 racing and it was very successful, notably as 914-6. The GT version with wider track, widened arches, different wheel/tyre ratio and more power was a real tool. A 914-6 privateer won the class at Le Mans in 1970.

of the Porsche passion at Prescott.

Owner's passion; it is about people not just cars and this 924 with appropriate ducting, wings and wheels proves the point on exiting another Porsche gathering.

Justin Mather is well known for taking his charged 924/944 Special (with Augment Automotive tweaking) up Prescott Hill Climb in very quick time. Seen here in 2018 with its 2.7-litres powering out of Paddock Bend to a 49.13 run and second place on the day, this car took the 2019 Porsche Club Speed Championship. The car also took FTD at Shelsley en route to the title.

924 Carrera GT race car in period as captured by Porsche at the height of its effect. (Photo: Porsche)

Above: 968CS on the go! Yellow delight at speed captures the excellence of 968 – another forgotten niche Porsche beyond 911 heaven. Think of the passion that went in to designing this car.

Left: Polyurethane Porsche parts amid the Devil's bread van? Not really. A 924 Carrera in black spools up for take-off.

Above: 968 out of 944 was a very fine car but again the narrative had its say. It looks scaled, organic, and timeless to the author, but you may disagree. Why do people misunderstand the Porsche process? This is a sleeper of an investment and a great car.

Right: The 'turret' of the Cayman cabin design captured as an earlier version speeds towards the camera. You cannot but help seeing shades of 356, Speedster and more here. Mid-engined, lithe and pointy, Cayman tracks true and is a great drive.

The more recent 718-series Spyder in the correct shade of silver and, on this occasion, gold-painted wheel that somehow look right; the vanes on the leading edge of the wheel arch reduce local aerodynamic lift acting on the front axle. The ducts in the bumper valance clean up the airflow into the wheels and axle area to reduce turbulence; modern Porsche design language at its best.

'*Enfant terrible*' to some, proper Porsche for the people according to others. Boxster probably saved Porsche and this lovely early Boxster looks just right cruising the countryside as a Porsche should. All the author knows is that if you are not of 'high-net worth', a cheap Boxster or sorted-out old 996 are your route to enjoying the driving of a Porsche.

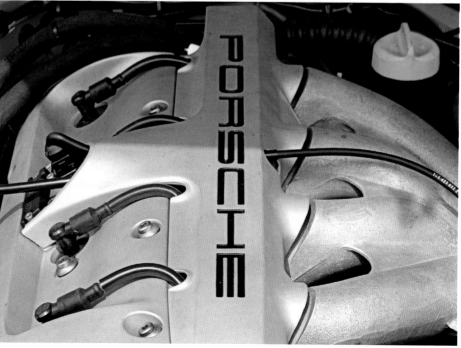

Above left: F.A. 'Butzi' Porsche at work. 'Porsche Design' was his industrial design company that went beyond cars and brilliant it was too. Porsche Design at Zell am See was a much missed member of the fraternity. (*Photo: Porsche*)

Above right: Anatole Carl 'Tony' Lapine (1930-2012) the Latvian-born Porsche designer. One of the greats of Porsche design. Stylish, colourfully opinionated, a race driver, a design-philosopher and a leader of what became 'design language'. He started out with Daimler-Benz, thence to Fisher and then General Motors in the USA (with input to various Corvette-related projects) then transferring to Opel prior to joining Porsche in 1969 and overseeing some of the most prolific periods of the Porsche design studio decades. Porsche fans owe him much. As they also do to Möbius, Söderberg, Lagaay, Sellar, Hatter, Murkett, and other Porsche designers. (*Photo: Porsche*)

Right: Signs of the times. Yet no different the configuration of other, earlier Porsches.

Ross McDonald powers out of Pardon as the gold Fuchs scrabble under Porsche power: this is one of those 911 moments of transcendental joy in 911 heaven. Is the accompanying music Beethoven, Brahms, or a Bach?

911 as the form sibylline – again. More, perfect, complex curves of ellipsoid axis and true sculpture. Has any car ever had such surreal form, being beyond fashion or passing motif?

Porsche has always done a nice line in blue. The back end of this 997 captures the way blue is the Porsche wavelength to be on.

Different strokes, the more recent GT3RS seen in elegant repose. You can still see that hallmark of design that goes back decades to Porsche's defining forms. The ducktail is somewhat overshadowed by that rear wing however.

Right: The cocoon: Porsche cockpits are always ergonomic and inspiring. Maybe a dark grey or back top roll might be a touch more restrained, but one thing is for sure, the interior of this car and its command post, has been *designed*.

Below: Ruf Ruf! A lovely Riviera Blue beast as modified. 911 with 445bhp, seen on the prowl with various addenda to create form, function and fun. KXI 930 says it all about the passion owners have for their steeds. This car of 1976 vintage was originally a 2.7-litre but now has genuine RUF 3.4 block with Mahle Motorsport forged pistons and the relevant K27 turbo. Everything has been 'blue-printed'— polished and perfected. The GT RSR rear wing signs off a long list of enthusiast's modifications that include a Riviera Blue engine fan! As for the Belfast registration plate, well that only adds to the allure does it not.

Above: Stuttgart's finest on a blue background. Somehow it is very fitting.

Above right and right: Even the factory has a thing about blue (or Blau). They like red, they like white, but blue does somehow have a Porsche feel to it. Prior to the launch of the very latest 992-series GT3, this GT2R was the real deal. As you can see the Porsche driver is hammering it hard. Note in the rear-view, the forward-lovely scoops on the engine cover. Perfection in the details – as usual. (*Photos: Porsche*)

Blue Class: An early 912 shows off its classic rump as it heads home. One of the greatest rear-aspects of a car design ever drawn – surely?

The emotion of that famous rear side-window design. A Riviera Blue 993 seen close-up. It is just perfectly scaled sculpture that was and remains unique.

Wolfgang Möbius (with Lapine) captured the Porsche heritage in the 928 —especially that rear aspect. Lapine later said that some Corvette styling themes had been of relevance.

Above: Entenbürzel . You know it makes sense. There is of course a 2.7 Flach-Six to be seen underneath.

Right: 'SU51 JET' on a 911 owned by the CEO of Cotswold Airport who also happens to drive a Turbo S Cabriolet. Suzannah Harvey does a lot for aviation and she somehow just managed to park her 911 in front of the very last British Airways 747-400 to leave Heathrow (LHR) and make the last ex- LHR landing (at Cotswold Airport) at the end of BA's 747 operational history. The airframe is in the 'Negus' BA100' retro-livery and set to become a tribute based at Cotswold Kemble Airport. Here is hoping Porsche Club GB can arrange to park a squadron of 911s under the wings and make a donation to the 747's upkeep.

Red with a black-bonnet and all the right bits: GT2RS on the prowl as only 911 can. (*Photo: Porsche*)

Every element of the 911 design shines here as the classic shape heads towards us. The car is a 912 by the way, and reeks of originality.

Above left: Then and now. Porsche branding on a Panamera's rump with 993 and 928 behind the behind.

Above right: Inside the spaceship; design as only Porsche can. A true sense of occasion upon entering the module. (*Photo: Porsche*)

Right: Whatever you think of electrickery, Taycan is beyond brilliant in its drive and its design. Quite how Porsche managed to make a 1930s streamliner look like a 2020s spaceship is another story, but every element of Porsche design from Ferdinand Porsche (Snr), with Erwin Komenda, Ferry Porsche, Butzi Porsche, and all the others, seems to have coalesced and amalgamated into more 'perfect' design with heritage that looks forward not back, and is retro but not a pastiche. This one is Gentian Blue and has real class. (*Photo: Porsche*)

Guard's red, big wheels, 991 storming along in blaze of passion.

Right: Walter Röhrl in the 959 and switching dynamics through the esses on a German road; memories of an icon. (*Photo: Porsche*)

Below: The exquisite Amalgam Model Collection's 1:8 scale 'model' of the lightweight 'Monza' 911. More perfection.

RennSport has many meanings. This RS has a roll-cage and 911 Rennsport nomenclature. It was about to race. Rennen metal indeed.

911S seen from above in blue. Light falls upon Porsche design legend.

More light falling upon metal: the early 901-series 911 (of recent 'Historika' operation) simply oozes *neun-elfer* ingredients as it passes the author's camera and provides essential encapsulation of the Porsche passion. One of the early-build cars and said to be the 180th built, this is short wheel base stuff of dreams for those of the 'early 911' persuasion.

Beethoven's Sixth? Porsche's 911; a 993 glides along in serene countryside as the elements sing. Porsche driving captured in different mood. '22 BAU' cruises home as the occupants are transported by delight.

'IIW 911' is a 1970-built 2.2 S in white with side-script and the correct Fuchs, and it is 911 heaven framed as the classic passion heads away from yet another gathering. We shall probably keep staring at Porsches for decades to come.

RSR flat-six, worship at the altar: lifting the lid on the Devil's delight of pure unadulterated 911 heaven. Ear plugs may be required and if you ask nicely Mr Howells might make it roar. *How* many horsepower did he say?

Index